Over the years, I have known Bill Donius as an artist, bank president, activist, and now as an extremely fine writer. *Thought Revolution: How to Unlock Your Inner Genius* is a brilliant new exploration of the power of the right brain and how it could change your life forever. Donius is a renaissance man and this book is just another piece of remarkable evidence of his genius.

—DAVID MIXNER, CIVIL RIGHTS ACTIVIST
AND BEST-SELLING AUTHOR

THOUGHT
REVOLUTION

HOW TO UNLOCK YOUR INNER GENIUS

WILLIAM A. DONIUS

CHANGING LIVES PRESS

Some of the names and locations in this book have been changed to protect the privacy of the individuals. The author of this book does not dispense medical or psychiatric advice, nor prescribe the use of any technique as a form of treatment for medical or psychiatric problems without the advice of a physician or therapist. This book contains general information and is not intended to be, nor should be, used as a substitution for specific medical advice.

Changing Lives Press
50 Public Square #1600
Cleveland, OH 44113
www.changinglivespress.com

Library of Congress Cataloging-in-Publication Data is available through the Library of Congress.

ISBN-13: 978-0-9843047-6-9 • ISBN 10: 0-9843047-6-2

Developmental editing and copywriting by
Bookchic, LLC • www.bookchic.net

Copyediting by Shari Johnson

Interior design & production by
The Book Couple • www.thebookcouple.com

Cover design by Nicholas N. Garza
www.NicholasNGarza.carbonmade.com

Printed in the United States of America

10   9   8   7   6   5   4   3   2   1

CONTENTS

PART TWO
LIFTING THE EIGHT LIES

For my parents,
Connie and Walter Donius

FOREWORD

THOUGHT REVOLUTION IS AN APT TITLE for William Donius's book because when you're through reading it, you will have widened the scope of the lens through which you view yourself and your life. If you have come to this book to help you better identify your feelings or tap into your intuition and creativity, you will not be disappointed.

The methods used in this book have proven effective for thousands of people worldwide for more than thirty years. I ought to know because I originated them. As demonstrated in hundreds of case studies presented in my fifteen books, the techniques you will learn in this book access the right brain and integrate the cerebral hemispheres, literally letting the left brain know what the right brain is doing. The result: the ability to use the whole brain to change your perceptions, actions, habits, and moods in revolutionary ways.

Bill's research and own eagerness to write this book came from his own success in utilizing both sides of his brain through the act of writing with his nondominant hand as a way of self-expression and introspection. What he discovered about himself will compel you to do the same. It's a thought evolution that acts as a Thought Revolution of the mind, which will connect each side of your brain in ways we have only been told possible.

There is exciting evidence I gathered while working with people of all walks of life that proves tapping your nondominant right brain can act as a direct pipeline to your inner truth, open up creative problem-solving abilities, and help you think outside the box. Others have reported improvements in relationships, reduction in stress, better physical health, discovery of hidden talents, deeper spiritual awareness, healing from trauma, breakthroughs in career, accessing inner wisdom, and connection with a higher power. And it all begins with moving the pencil from one hand to the other.

I can pay Bill no higher compliment than to say he "walks his talk." Beyond his many achievements in the world of business and finance, Bill's best credential for writing this book is that he applied the techniques he writes about to his own life and experienced a transformation. What Bill discovered was that there are eight lies that we commonly tell ourselves, and he uncovered them when he began writing with his nondominant hand.

In *Thought Revolution* Bill sets out to help us under-stand the science behind why we tell ourselves lies, which side of the brain is to blame, and the methods to use to blast them from our consciousness in order to find—and live—our truth. Bill expands on the method by focusing on uncovering outworn beliefs and atti-tudes and turning them around to replace them with new thought processes that can change our lives. And what could be more practical than to shed that which no longer serves us? Like the little boy in *The Emperor's New Clothes*, Bill demystifies familiar "untruths" and helps us free ourselves from their powerful grip.

After working with one of my books, *Recovery of Your Inner Child*, for many years, Bill found me on the Internet. What can I say? Our first phone conversation lasted for two hours! He sent me the manuscript, and I was utterly fascinated. I performed each exercise and discovered how susceptible I had been to these common lies. The results were fast and dramatic. After eating, sleeping, and breathing these techniques for years, I was introduced to yet another application in daily life. As you will learn, this is indicative of how even my own patterns had become so ingrained that they prevented me from working "outside the box." What a delight to be given my own "medicine," this time by another adventurer to the inner world.

Never before has there been greater receptivity to applications of brain research for dealing with day-to-day challenges and life issues. Brain research has mushroomed in the years since Dr. Roger W. Sperry won a Nobel Prize in 1981 for his pioneering work into hemispheric functions. The notoriety of Jill Bolte Taylor's book *My Stroke of Insight,* which details her experience of the right brain while having a stroke in the left hemisphere, has set the stage for books like the one you are about to read.

After doing all the exercises in Part Two of this book, I can attest that Bill's book delivers on its promise: You can change the way you think and find your truth in whatever challenges you. Whether you are recovering from a trauma, grappling with a life-altering decision, fighting to lose weight, or searching for a romantic relationship, *Thought Revolution* will take you on a journey that will set you free.

—Lucia Capacchione, Ph.D., ATR (Art Therapist Registered), and author of *Recovery of Your Inner Child* and *The Power of the Other Hand*

PART ONE

STOP LYING, START LIVING

ONE

TAKING BETTER ADVANTAGE
OF THE *WHOLE* MIND

D O YOU SOMETIMES FEEL LIKE a laboratory animal lost in a maze as you pursue life, success, and happiness? Try this little experiment. Take a blank piece of paper. At the top, write the question:

If I were an animal, what animal would I be?

Take a few seconds to clear your mind. Now write down your answer. Switch your pen or pencil to the other hand and don't switch it back. Reread the question you wrote at the top of the page. Take a deep breath and let your lungs expand. Remember, this is an experiment. Suspend judgment about how your handwriting will look or whether you'll be able to do it. Trust yourself and allow your nondominant hand to write its answer to the question. Put your writing instrument down on top of the paper . . . and read on.

We go through life wounded by various negative experiences. We heal from these experiences and develop emotional scar tissue. Similar to the child who gets burned by touching something on a hot stove, we get tougher and learn to avoid certain topics and issues as we grow. The good news is we keep ourselves emotionally safe from potential trauma. The bad news is we close ourselves off to risk taking. Consequently, we are more cautious and less interested in going in a new direction involving risk, especially if attached to a topic that has "burned" us previously. Most of the time, we end up staying within the confines of the life we have created for ourselves. We abandon the idea of risk in order to get what we really want out of life.

We can learn to tap into a broader range of our thought processes. These thoughts are always present but often get shut down immediately because of past experiences in which we learned to protect ourselves from danger. Certainly, we don't want to unlearn what has kept us safe from harm, nor do we want to stay stuck in risk-negative behaviors keeping us from reaching our true potential in life. How do we achieve a healthy balance?

This book explores how we arrive at various *limiting positions in life*. I call these the *lies we tell ourselves*. I believe these lies are perpetuated in our left brain by the dominant linear thinking style of our left brain.

Life can be the experience of what we came here to

learn, or it can become what we choose to suppress. We have a choice. But it takes courage to act, to become aware, to be intentional about what we do in life. This book is about helping you find a place of inner peace and wisdom that will allow you to discover the steps you need to take to find the greatest amount of meaning in your life. It may even ignite a revolution in your traditional thought process.

We have an opportunity to reach our true potential; however, we must be purposeful and intentional about getting where we want to go—making the changes necessary to unravel the ties that bind us. *Thought Revolution* will help focus your intentionality of purpose in life.

If you think I'm the leader of the pack who has all the answers to your questions about life, success, and happiness, you're dead wrong. Still, I've learned a few things, and you may find them helpful. The experiment on page 3 could be the beginning of any number of lessons you can learn. I know it's taught me a lot about myself. I've also watched it start many of my friends and acquaintances on the road to important discoveries about themselves. Consider it a preview to equally fascinating exercises provided in Part Two of this book.

Since humankind climbed down from the trees, we have looked for ways to improve our circumstances. Maybe we want a better environment to live in, more suitable people to relate to, or more gratifying work. In any case, we think and scheme constantly about how we can better spend the short but precious time we have on earth. When we are lucky and blessed, we occasionally make a little progress along the path through life. Other times, though, we feel thwarted and blocked.

In my life, I've noticed that sometimes a veil obscures my vision of the solutions I know ought to be right in front of me. For me, procrastination is the perfect example of me getting in my own way. I don't like the pressure of having to crank out some project because the due date is uncomfortably close. Yet, absurdly, many times in my life I find myself back in exactly the same uncomfortable spot. It's a pattern I just couldn't break, no matter how conscious I was of its detrimental effects on my psyche and my work. And we all have patterns—some positive, some negative. Our good intentions tell us, usually at New Year's or on our birthdays, that we will change our minds—change the way our brains operate to experience a new way of living that will enhance our decision making and positively affect our choices. We understand that we must first recognize our patterns in order to break them. But it's easier said than done, and we often find ourselves—as I did with procrastination—back where we started. Why are our brains so seemingly stuck and difficult to change?

THE AMAZE-ING MIND

The brain is like a maze in which our patterns of behavior are lab mice scurrying through, hunting for the proverbial bit of cheese—goals and desires. When we achieve the desired aim of our behavior, we think, "Aha! That's what I was looking for. I've got to remember the path I followed to get here because I know I'm going to want some more of this excellent cheese later!"

After lunch, the scientist puts us back at the beginning of the maze and lets us go again. Scurry, scurry, scurry, and we get the cheese a second time! Repeat the test again; the mouse learns the lesson almost perfectly. In fact, if you change the type of cheese that is placed at the end of the maze, the mouse will eventually run the maze it learned by habit, without caring if the cheese is to its preference or existent at all. Humans do the same thing. Once we plot a route that produces results, we habitually go about that route no matter what is there waiting for us. For the most part, we get very used to any repeated process. The tunnels, the turns, the switchbacks and straightaways begin to feel like home. Over time, the pattern of the maze becomes completely familiar. Then, the learned patterns and approaches to conflicts, problems, or solutions become so ingrained that we fail to see any other possible way . . . cheese or no cheese.

But here is the kicker: Once we get to the end of our maze, no matter what is there waiting for us as a result of our habitual pattern, or route, we will tell ourselves that is what we wanted, or worse, what we deserved. We literally lie to ourselves to cover up the disappointment because we crave inner peace. It's easier to believe the lie than face the truth.

We save face by convincing ourselves that we didn't settle for the wrong significant other when we are pining for a lost love, or that we are in the right job when we keep getting passed over for promotions. What about when we tell ourselves we deserve to be trampled on by family members or used by friends; that we are lesser than everybody else and should be happy with what we have? Does any of this sound familiar? It's tough to invest time, emotion, and some-times money in ventures that turn out to produce a less-than-desired outcome, so doesn't it make sense to preserve our egos by lying to ourselves? "Of course this is what I wanted," or "This isn't exactly what I planned, but it's better than nothing."

These are only a few of the lies we tell ourselves. In fact, through researching brain science and writing with our nondominant hand, I have identified eight common lies we tell ourselves when we are trapped in the mind maze described here. This book will demonstrate reasons why we tell ourselves various lies and explore why we have a vested interest in *believing these lies*. We will also explore what actions we can take to be able to make progress in *breaking through these limitations* so we have a better chance of realizing our full potential in life. We need to jump out of the maze when the cheese goes missing.

MY STORY

How would I know? I offer myself as Exhibit A. I was

the prototypical, right-handed, left-brained, linear, logical thinker. For thirty years, these traits helped me climb the corporate ladder until I reached the top rung as chairman and CEO of a public company. For over a dozen years, I ran a very successful bank. Surely, banking is the epitome of rational and logical business. Everything has to make sense. I mean, literally, it must all add up or the bank closes its doors!

Although my rational mind was a terrific asset in my career, I found it much less helpful when I needed to resolve issues in my personal life. I felt way too much like the guy who keeps doing the same thing over and over expecting a different result each time. But my problems were unavoidable. Even procrastination couldn't put off attending to them forever.

What to do? Faced with serious roadblocks in my personal life, I was tempted to focus only on those parts of my life where I succeeded, and I did so for a decade or more. My career proceeded unhampered, no matter how confusing my personal life. Yes, my myriad successes and the perks and spoils of my job gratified me. But as much as I enjoyed them, they ultimately did not content me. After reaching a sense of desperation—an emptiness that kept me unfulfilled and alone—I decided I had to face the personal issues or else risk a life of perpetual unhappiness.

Finally, I took the issues to my psychotherapist, who recommended I read Lucia Capacchione's breakthrough book, *Recovery of Your Inner Child*. That book made me understand that the part of myself I suppressed—the part that was not running a bank, but failing in intimate relationships and creative expression—lived in my underactive, underdeveloped, and underutilized "right brain." It was the part of my brain that was not satisfied with the lack of cheese at the end of my maze, but was told lies to ease the disappointment. I did not want to settle for Kraft Singles when I might be able to have aged Gouda. My right brain was suffering, and I needed to tend to it in order to heal it and discover my truth.

I was spending fifty to seventy hours a week on work, so I began activating my right brain by writing with my nondominant left hand by posing the question, "How can I achieve better balance in life?"

The answer I wrote with my left hand was, "You could spend less time on work-related pursuits and accept fewer work-related activities or projects; reserve at least two or three nights a week as Bill time."

Although, this may not seem like an incredible insight, it was very helpful for me at the time. I stopped taking on additional projects and devoted more time to my pursuits. As you will discover when it's your turn to partake in the nondominant hand exercises, oftentimes the insights we uncover may seem obvious to outsiders, but not to us.

By exploring my right brain through writing with my nondominant left hand, I learned to access the place where I had locked some memories tightly away. After a time I was able to unlock some of my own mysteries and break through barriers that had stymied me for decades. The solution for me involved learning how to set loose material I had repressed, and when I did, I gained the insights into who I really am and the things I truly desire. I'll share more about these insights in Part Two. The technique I used to achieve this breakthrough involved posing a series of questions, prompts, and drawing exercises to myself and using my nondominant hand to answer them. I call this process "intuitive writing" or "right-brain writing," and will use these terms interchangeably throughout the book. As weird as it felt to my ordinarily rational mind, the process has proved to be revolutionary and transformational in my life.

What I found particularly extraordinary was how naturally the process of personal change came through intuitive writing. Once my subconscious right brain was unblocked and a pathway was created to the left brain, my old habits and ways of thinking moved aside to make room for the new approaches suggested by the right brain. Scientists are still not exactly certain about how this process works. However, in my personal experience the thought or idea that is jogged from activation of the right brain can instantly feel like a really good one—intuitively and instinctually. The messages from the right brain are recognized and then validated by the whole mind as good ideas—like a "light bulb going on"—which supports the power of the subconscious mind. Perhaps the question we pose to our right brain is answered and accepted so readily because the truth has been lingering in the deep recesses of

A NOTE TO LEFTIES

Intuitive writing works equally well for left-handed and right-handed people. Generally the left hemisphere controls the right side of the body, and the right controls the left side of the body, so it is a common belief that a left-handed person exhibits more right brain traits, i.e., creativity, and right-handed people are stronger in left-brain abilities, i.e., analysis. These generalizations lead us to the false assumption that left-handers, then, are already in tune with their subconscious "right brains," or at least more than their righty counterparts. But scientists have discovered that the right brain is the less dominant hemisphere regardless of hand dominance, and that nondominant hand writing allows a person—left or righty—to tap into the right subconscious mind.

Here's another twist, my neuroscientist friend, David Freedman, Ph.D., a professor at the Department of Neurobiology at the University of Chicago, points out that in many left-handed people, language centers are found in the right hemisphere. This suggests in those subjects, "right brain" creative thinking may actually be handled by the left hemisphere.

It's important to note that there are scientific limits to our understanding of the brain, including understanding how functions are lateralized in the brain. As of the writing of this book, two scientific research projects on the lateralization of brain functions are scheduled to commence in my hometown of St. Louis, Missouri, and Chicago.

the mind for a long time. Therefore, on some level, what we unlock is not foreign to us after all.

Today I'm generally a more balanced thinker. I make better personal decisions. I can now draw fairly equally from my innate style of rational, linear thinking, while not neglecting sparks of creativity, insight, and intuition that reside in parts of my right brain that I didn't use effectively before. I apply different techniques today, and my creativity has blossomed. I can think "outside the box" about issues at work as well as at home and possess a "big picture" view about my life. My thought revolution prohibits me from telling myself lies, so I can stay in pursuit of my truths.

Before we can get to this payoff, I will need to set the stage by addressing the roles our left and right brain play in the way we think about what is possible in our lives. I will offer techniques and processes to evaluate potential opportunities in a new light. My goal is to help you make better decisions by taking advantage of your whole mind. I have intentionally oversimplified the manner in which the left and right brain work by calling it "Left Brain Lies, Right Brain Answers." In fact, you will be using both hemispheres of your brain as you work through the prescribed steps. The information you get from this process will literally be *pulled from your brain.* This is where it gets really interesting.

TWO

OF TWO MINDS:
A RELATIVELY RECENT
DISCOVERY

THE THREE-POUND CRUMPLED LOOKING thing in our head we know as our brain is still one of the most complicated. The typical brain consists of some 100 billion cells, each of which communicates with up to 10,000 of its colleagues. Together they forge an elaborate network of some quadrillion (1,000,000,000,000,000) connections guiding how we talk, eat, breathe, and move. James Watson, who won the Nobel Prize for helping discover DNA, described the human brain as the "most complex thing we have yet discovered in our universe."

In the 1950s, Cal Tech professor Roger Sperry reshaped our understanding of the human brain. He studied patients who had epileptic seizures that had required removal of the corpus callosum, the thick bundle of some 300 million nerve fibers that connects the brain's two hemispheres. In a set of experiments on these "split brain" patients, Sperry discovered the established view was flawed. Yes, our brains were divided into two halves, but, as he put it, "the subordinate, or minor hemisphere, which we had formerly supposed to be the illiterate and mentally retarded one and thought by some authorities to not even be conscious, was found to be in fact the superior cerebral member when it came to performing certain kinds of mental tasks."

Sperry demonstrated the right hemisphere of the brain was not inferior to the left. It was just different. Sperry wrote, "There appear to be two modes of thinking represented rather separately in the left and right hemispheres, respectively." The left hemisphere reasoned sequentially, excelled at analysis and handled words. The right hemisphere reasoned holistically recognized patterns and interpreted emotions and nonverbal expressions. Human beings were literally of two minds.

Neuroscientist Joseph Bogen wrote in *Brain Circuits and Functions of the Mind*, "The implications of this [Sperry's] work have yet to be fully appreciated. The principle of hemispheric specialization (left: language; right: spatial abilities) illuminated by him, has been widely recognized, which has stimulated an immense amount of research. But the principle of cerebral duality (that each hemisphere has its own mind) has so far had insufficient recognition. . . . We all look forward to the day when the implications of the split-brain research emerge in a form that can help guide human society toward an improved understanding of its own internally conflicted creativity."

In Betty Edwards's 1979 pivotal book, *Drawing on the Right Side of the Brain,* Sperry's work was applied to her own theory that anyone can learn to draw. "Drawing is not that difficult," she maintained. "Seeing is the problem." Edwards's book teaches techniques for being able to "see better" by learning to quiet the "know it all, loud" left brain, so the quieter, creative right brain can do its thing.

Evolutionary theory states we are born into this world as the genetic product of our parents and those who came before them. Neuroscientist David Freedman, Ph.D, explained to me that our molecular, chemical circuit connections and overall architecture of the brain are inherited and established by our genes. As soon as we are born, we are influenced by all the environmental factors around us, including our parents' behaviors as well as the influences of siblings, friends, teachers, etc. Our right brain is a predetermined genetic calculation by our parents' DNA. Yet, our left brain is heavily influenced by environmental factors.

Scientists don't believe the right and left brains operate as on-off switches—one powering down as soon as the other lights up. Both halves play a role in nearly everything we do. In *The Dana Guide to Brain Health,* doctors Bloom, Beal, and Kupfer wrote, "We can say certain regions of the brain are more active than others when it comes to certain functions, but we can't say those functions are confined to particular areas."

RIGHTY, LEFTY. WHAT'S THE DIFFERENCE?

In *A Whole New Mind*, Daniel Pink summarizes the plethora of research on the two hemispheres of the brain by identifying four key differences:

1. **The left hemisphere controls the right side of the body; the right hemisphere controls the left side of the body.** Since 90 percent of the population is right handed, it means that in roughly 90 percent of the population the left hemisphere is controlling the important movements such as handwriting, eating, and maneuvering a computer mouse.

2. **The left hemisphere is sequential; the right hemisphere is simultaneous.** The right hemisphere does not march in the single-file formation of A-B-C-D-E. It is specialized in seeing many things at once, seeing all the elements of a situation and understanding what they mean.

3. **The left hemisphere specializes in text; the right hemisphere specializes in context.** The left hemisphere handles what is said, the right hemisphere focuses on how it is said—the nonverbal, often emotional cues delivered through a gaze, facial expression, and intonation.

4. **The left hemisphere analyzes the details; the right hemisphere synthesizes the big picture.** The left focuses on categories, the right on relationships. The left can grasp the details. But only the right hemisphere can see the big picture.

Neuroscientists agree the right and left brains take different paths regarding the way in which we interpret and think about the world.

LEFT BRAIN LIES, RIGHT BRAIN ANSWERS: UNDERSTANDING THE RELATIONSHIP

We learn at an early age we get praise for that which we demonstrate proficiency. This praise, combined with the actual proficiency, gives the brain a strong message: this type of activity should be reinforced when possible. This is called the positive feedback loop. It is a very comforting place for the brain, psyche, and body to inhabit. This loop produces pleasant feelings and sensations throughout the body. We learn at an early age that these types of feelings—provoked by the left brain—are desirable, even though the impulse for the idea may be from the right brain. Scientists are now using brain scans to better understand where thoughts originate in our brains. Scanning systems allow this to happen in real time. If we are asked to think about our mother, scientists are able to view the various places in the brain that are active and engaged by this thought process.

The left brain acts as a guard to ensure we continue to experience stimuli that give us pleasure, or at least minimize pain. Our right brain is content to stay passively in the background and allow the left brain to run the show. My hunch, after hundreds of interviews with test subjects, is the right brain contains more of what makes us who we are, including our personality. There is no scientific evidence yet, however, about how this works.

We also learn there are risks when we consciously or unconsciously expose who we are to others. This may happen on the school playground when kids call each other names. Generally, the terms are derogatory: sissy, nerd, brownnoser, etc. We learn early on this type of name-calling causes a negative feeling in our brain, psyche, and body. We learn that we want to avoid this feeling. This is called the negative feedback loop. Our left brain, and specifically our left prefrontal cortex, might be involved in controlling this kind of complex reasoning as well as emotional responses to act as a buffer or protector to keep this type of information from getting through and causing us to feel pain. As mentioned in Chapter 1, we accumulate a sort of emotional scar tissue, and the sum total of these two responses is pretty clear: we develop a pattern in life for doing what brings us pleasure and avoiding what hurts.

Do our brains get locked into this process for life, or can we break the cycle? This cycle can quite easily become our primary operating system if we are not actively engaged in reprogramming the brain. For the brain to be reprogrammed, we must be in a place where the right brain can get the nourishment it needs —such as a loving, encouraging family atmosphere. It is specifically the right brain that is more vulnerable and therefore needs a safety zone so it can act without fear of negative reprisal or the negative feedback loop.

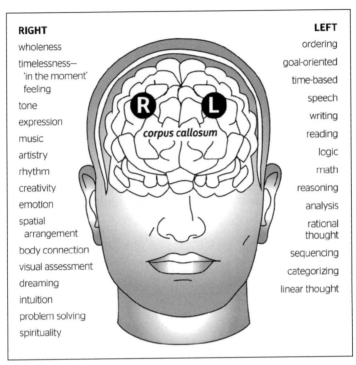

RIGHT

wholeness

timelessness—
'in the moment'
feeling

tone

expression

music

artistry

rhythm

creativity

emotion

spatial
arrangement

body connection

visual assessment

dreaming

intuition

problem solving

spirituality

LEFT

ordering

goal-oriented

time-based

speech

writing

reading

logic

math

reasoning

analysis

rational
thought

sequencing

categorizing

linear thought

corpus callosum

Brain Functions of the Two Hemispheres

This is often why young musicians develop faster and better when their parents are musicians. They have both the DNA and the social factors working for them as they get the praise and nurturing the brain requires in order to continue with an activity.

NATURE AND NURTURE

Actors' kids are more likely to find acting or performing easier than children of non-thespians. I'm sure I had an easier time beginning a career as a banker at age thirty-two because both my grandfather and father were bankers. I felt learning the business came far easier to me than other pursuits. I worked over a thirteen-year period after business school in the fields of public relations, high-tech healthcare sales, and television production. When it came to banking I found an immediate sense of familiarity. This begs the classic genetics versus environmental question. Was my own familiarity in banking due to my genetic makeup or observing my father and grandfather in the banking environment?

The answer, of course, is both. There is not a great deal I remember of my father talking about the banking business growing up. Further, I never really saw him at work being a banker like the musician's son would see his father perform. I really only saw him reading and working out of his briefcase when he came home from work.

Given these facts, perhaps my comfort with banking had more to do with DNA? There is one important exception: I did witness the positive feedback my father received from being a banker. I got the message early on that this was a good career for him. My takeaway was banking might also work for me. Since the left brain wants to guard and protect us, this was a valuable message to receive in childhood. The right brain became engaged decades later when I actually started working as a banker. It was a feeling I can do this. It was a stronger sense than I had at other jobs.

This is certainly a great feeling to have. Ultimately, it's one the body craves as well as the mind. We want and need a sense of order and purpose in our lives. The lucky ones are those who are in this zone, where they experience the peace and serenity that comes with being in the right place at the right time. This allows both the right and left brains to feel a sense of balance and peace.

The right brain is fulfilled when it is allowed to draw upon its vast database and capabilities. The left brain gets a sense of purpose when it is able to take part in activities satisfying the body's needs. It is also comforting for the left brain to systematically approach tasks and processes for which it gets positive feedback. When it comes to the workplace, both our left and right brains can be activated, engaged, and at peace in the appropriate job.

Unfortunately, the opposite happens when either our left or right brain is not activated or engaged. Instead of being at peace, we are in turmoil. This typically happens when the right brain is not engaged in the work process. There can be angst and frustration taking place because the right brain does not feel it is fulfilling its true purpose or it is not being tapped adequately.

Underwhelm infects the left brain, leaving it feeling restless and in turmoil. In turn, a message is sent that it should accordingly send warning signs to provoke a change in behavior. However, this provokes a conflict: the left brain is primarily concerned with preserving the status quo and creating an environment safe for the occupant. Of course, the stakes are much higher if the occupant is also providing for a family or running a company in which there are implied responsibilities to the employees and their families.

TO OUR HEMISPHERE'S DISCONTENT

When there is a disagreement between the left and right brains, there is inherent conflict between what is in the best interest of the occupant. In these types of wars, it is usually the left brain that wins, as it is the primary operating system responsible for day-to-day functions. The right brain is more of the primary thinking/processing system and still must process those thoughts (or clear them) through the left brain.

Since the left brain is the primary operating system within most of us, it gets a certain veto power. This veto power may limit us and manifest itself as a lie that the left brain devises to presumably "protect" us from what it does not think the conscious mind should hear. All of this happens so fast in our brain—the world's most complicated processing and operating system— that we are barely aware it has happened at all.

It is important to get to the place where we feel we are accomplishing our life's purpose. When we get to this place, we truly feel as if we are making progress along our path in life. This feeling is clearly a good one because it produces a great feeling in both parts of our brain.

What happens when we feel we are not on the right path? When we have that sinking feeling things are not right? This feeling is caused by the right brain sending a signal that we are not doing what is in our highest and best interest. When we get this feeling, we can either quickly dismiss the thought or—if it continues to nag at us—we can choose to tell ourselves a lie that dismisses the thought without us feeling bad or guilty about it.

"The paradox of prosperity is while living standards have risen steadily decade after decade, personal, family, and life satisfaction haven't budged," says Columbia University's Andrew Delbanco, author of *The Real American Dream: A Meditation on Hope.* "That's why more people—liberated by prosperity but not fulfilled by it—are resolving the paradox by searching for meaning."

Delbanco adds, "The most striking feature of contemporary culture is the craving for transcendence." I know I am a great deal more satisfied now that I have the time to pursue my interests and the items on my bucket list. Choosing to retire early from corporate America means I essentially had to buy my freedom by accepting a lower annual income. The tradeoff is certainly worth it for me.

I know of a very successful senior-level banker who wanted to be an attorney, but to bury the discontent of not following through with her goals, she lies to herself by saying it's not practical to go back to law school at age thirty-seven. In so doing, she lets herself off the hook. I also know a banker who wanted to be a journalist. He told himself at a young age he might not be good enough to make it as a journalist, so pursuing a business degree would be much more practical. He had a successful career in banking, but constantly wonders, "What if?"

The left brain craves the status quo. So it is unlikely to allow us to give serious consideration to a major life change. Since we depend on our left brain to guide us through these changes, we cannot discount the thought process we get from it. Ironically, these thoughts can come in the form of warning signs influencing us to change our mind from thinking about a specific idea any further.

Most of the world operates in a left-brain framework, as it is both logical and easier to operate from

AN INTERESTING THOUGHT

The phrase "I changed my mind" may derive from a reference to a thought that originated in the right brain and then crossed over to the left brain for its "approval." The crossover and how the idea is transformed once it lands in the left brain cause us to feel as if we have truly "changed our mind." In fact, we have. More accurately, we could state that we "changed our brain" on the topic.

this place. However, there is a great deal that can be missed along the way because we are limiting the creative, intuitive right brain from operating at anything close to full capacity. Consequently, we consistently limit our potential for authentic successes in life. I define this type of success as that which gives us the most satisfaction in life. This does not necessarily mean the type of success that will make us the most money, although often there is a strong correlation between what we enjoy doing and the type of work that brings us the best financial payout.

Lying is a form of self-preservation.

The link is not always immediate. Consider the individual who decides to do standup comedy. It takes years perhaps to get to a point where it is a financially viable means of support. Another example is artists who take a long time to get to a point where their work sells to a degree where it can be a full-time pursuit.

Often the left brain gets involved and slows down the process. We may tell ourselves, "I'm not good enough" or "this will take too long," and thereby end up slowing down the process and the previous positive trajectory. We must learn to recognize, evaluate, and stop ourselves from telling these and a variety of other lies. In the coming pages, you will learn how to identify *when* you are lying to yourself and *how* to stop.

THREE

A CONVERSATION WITH YOUR RIGHT BRAIN

THERE IS A TEMPTATION TO BELIEVE that at a certain stage in life we are set on our course and there is not much we can do to change it. That means we don't have to put ourselves through some sort of personal hell or turmoil attempting to figure out what we are supposed to do with the rest of our lives. In fact, this is effectively a left-brain deception tactic.

It is convenient for our linear left brain to subscribe to this belief. If it is okay to stay on the same path we've been on for the past two, five, ten, or twenty years, it makes life a lot easier. If risk is introduced, we will no longer be satisfied with the path, the direction, or possibly the journey itself.

These moments of reflection can be difficult and scary to us. It is similar to hanging with a best friend who is a negative influence. Despite this fact, he is still our friend. And we don't necessarily want to break off the friendship. I suppose the same dynamic is true to a far greater degree when we are in an intimate relationship as an adult that is not fulfilling. It is difficult to break out of a long-held, familiar pattern.

Why do we stick with these patterns, relationships, and friends—especially if they are not working for us? We conform to these patterns because we fear we will be lost without them. We don't like the thought of standing alone without a plan. That notion is really scary to us. Therefore, we would rather stay in a relationship or stay in a job or setting, even if substandard, than consider a change. It is difficult to comprehend as a concept, but I'm sure we can think of personal examples that apply.

The reason is we get conditioned by the logical left brain to protect what we have. There is a great deal of value placed on the here and now. The left brain is extremely risk averse, as it is concerned with ensuring we keep food on the table and a roof over our heads. Anything that potentially threatens our security is avoided. We can observe this when we sometimes literally begin to shut down as we consider what alternatives exist for us outside our present circumstances. This helps to reinforce an investment in the collective status quo. When we drift into opportunities where we can use our right brain, we may feel overwhelmed. Or, when we meet people who operate from a right brain perspective, we may think of them as odd.

Our brain is a very complex organ. Scientists know the brain to be an evolutionary marvel as it has kept our species alive for a long time. The brain works in a holistic manner that has served us very well. Yet, at times our brain doesn't seem to serve us as well we would like. We get stuck, make mistakes, or run from the obstacles and barriers that come our way.

We can use the techniques in this book to make progress in getting insight into our lives by tapping into instincts, ideas, and ideology we may not have been previously aware of. I believe we can learn a great deal by activating the right brain to gain the wisdom available to us. We can learn to think differently. We can ignite right brain creativity to cause a revolution in our thought process. Beginning right now.

AN INTRODUCTION TO INTUITIVE WRITING

If you didn't attempt the animal exercise in Chapter 1, do it now.

If I were an animal, what animal would I be?

Take a few seconds to clear your mind. Now write down your answer. Next, draw a line across the page below what you've written. Switch your pen or pencil to the other hand, and don't switch it back. Reread the question you wrote at the top of the page. Take a deep breath and let your lungs expand. Remember, this is an experiment. Suspend judgment about how your hand-writing will look or whether you'll be able to succeed in the exercise. Trust yourself, and allow your non-dominant hand to write its answer to the question.

"If I were an animal, what animal would I be?" Ask yourself whether you're resisting something. You've got nothing to lose. Take the risk. Open yourself to the power and advantages of your whole mind.

In almost every case, people get answers from the nondominant hand that are completely different from the answer they thought through and wrote down the first time. Is that what happened to you when you did the exercise? When participants reflect on the two answers, most are surprised because they have no idea where their second answer came from. Dogs, cats, horses, and birds are the most common dominant-hand answers. Nondominant-hand answers vary dramatically. I've gotten responses that range from porcupine to snake, walrus to platypus, and dolphin to great white shark. Clearly, when we give the creative right brain some room to play, it works in amazing ways.

One question that generates two answers happens because switching from dominant to nondominant hand activates the passageway into the right brain and unleashes its more intuitive thinking. In the process, it reveals that two relatively independent consciousnesses exist in the brain. After assisting hundreds of interview subjects with this question, I have formed a hypothesis about why most people write different responses to the same question. In the "animal" exercise, I characterize the dominant hand's response as an "aspirational" definition of oneself. The sort of response that would logically come from the rational side of the mind reflects one's conscious intentions or aspirations. But the nondominant hand seems to turn the table. Its response elicits a more "representational" animal that is more descriptive of how the person may function in everyday life.

The right brain, in my opinion, is more intuitively able to select what animal we are more closely aligned with based on behavior or attributes. The animal that is typically a closer *representation* of a person's "being" is the one written by the nondominant hand, and without prior conscious thought.

I'll use my mother as an example to expand on my hunch. When posed the question, "If I were an animal, what animal would I be?" my mother's dominant hand answered "dog." Her nondominant hand answer, however, was "tiger." We both laughed after she wrote "tiger" because it is actually a much better representation of how she functions. After all, she was the mother of three wild kids who were close in age, and she ruled the jungle protectively, with no reservation about speaking her mind. A dog, after all, doesn't roar.

In contrast, my mother's "aspirational" self was described as a dog. My mother's intent and aspirations in life on a conscious (left-brain) level could be said to work hard "like a dog," while also be a loving and loyal companion to her husband and protector to her children. And both sides of her brain were right. She is both dog and tiger, but she is a little more acquainted with her full persona now that she has recognized the attributes of her subconscious mind.

In another case, at a lecture I delivered, a professor from a prestigious school wrote "dog" (one of the most common answers) followed by "giraffe." He shared that he had no earthly idea why he wrote "giraffe." Fortunately, his wife was in the audience and stated, "That makes a lot of sense to me. You've always been the one to see and discover what others have been unable to. Just like the giraffe has the ability to see and reach places other animals cannot."

When a person's responses vary dramatically between the two hands, the creative part of the mind seems to conduct a nearly instantaneous scan of the personality and suggests the type of animal that represents the person. As you analyze your responses, ask yourself if the aspirational/representational dichotomy is true for you. If you're in doubt, think about what characteristics you share with each of the animals. Write down your answers using your nondominant hand. Are you more like the first or second animal? Based on the people I've sampled, I bet you'll decide that the second animal is a better self-representation than the first. I've labeled the second answer the "inner animal" since it seems to reveal some inner wisdom not revealed by the dominant hand. Could your right mind know you better than you thought? At the very least, something quite interesting and unusual happens in the brain when someone can so effortlessly derive two answers to the same question within thirty seconds of one another.

The scientific community has inspired me to take this work further by setting up a more traditional research context to learn more about what is occurring in the brain during my animal exercise when questions are answered separately by the dominant and nondominant hands. I'm hopeful to work with scientists and researchers to design experiments with the appropriate controls to validate the answers obtained.

FOUR

MAPPING THE
LABYRINTH

OBTAIN A JOURNAL OR SOME OTHER BLANK BOOK to designate as your own *Thought Revolution Journal.* Write the title in the middle of the first page. Or, if you have a smart phone, scan this QR code for a link to a sample journal. Now, locate your responses to the animal question from Chapter 1. Tuck that into the second page of the journal. Then, at the top of page three, write the question:

How do I feel about being playful and "acting like a kid"?

Answer the question with your nondominant hand. Close the book for today.

It will seem odd to attempt to write with your nondominant hand. You will discover it is possible, although it may not be easy at first as the letters and words come out painfully slow.

The premise behind using the nondominant hand is not simply trying to succeed at some sort of physical contortion by being able to do something we don't typically do (or perhaps never even attempted). Instead, the premise is that we are using a procedure to help us add to the traditional left-brain thought process by introducing a new way to access the right brain.

The purpose is to stimulate the creative, right brain into thinking without immediate and certain intervention from the more practical left brain. By changing our standard practice, we are more likely to get a different result. For this process to work, we must be willing to suspend disbelief. If we are able to keep an open mind, this exercise can and will work for us. This is a critically important aspect of being able to do this exercise. Our intent is to awaken the genius within, not bring upon madness.

The next step is being able to pose a question to the right brain for consideration. The objective is to ensure you actively involve your right brain in the brainstorming data dump.

Since the right brain is not as developed when it comes to language and therefore not as accessible to most of us, we may not be able to benefit from the thoughts and ideas residing in the right brain unless we specifically cultivate or pose questions to the more creative right brain.

I encourage you to approach this book and everything you write in it as a form of play, or at least as a break from work and the demands of our busy lives. If you are a Monty Python fan you may want to consider the famous refrain, "And now for something completely different," as you take out your *Thought Revolution Journal*. Things you eventually write here may reveal some of the most serious self-discoveries you will ever make, but the journey you're embarking on should make you feel like a wondrous child. If you can't sense enormous anticipation and imagine this as potentially "the opportunity of a lifetime," or "your personal revolution," you won't stick it out and see it through to the end.

When you begin writing, you may not be sure of what you are writing or why. Be patient and allow the process to occur. You may write only a sentence or two. Since it is new and unfamiliar, it may seem strange. Just allow it to transpire without judgment. After you are finished writing, go back and reread what surfaced. You may find that by engaging your right brain, you've written something previously expressed or you may surprise yourself by discovering a revolutionary new thought or idea.

Through this process, my hope is for you to unlock messages your right brain wants you to know. Some describe the right brain as more closely linked to the higher self or the god within. It seems to have a direct pipeline to the soul through the heart and is not concerned about ego, others, or the world we live in. The simple, profound words are often clear, specific, and come with an age-old wisdom. These messages can have a transformational, revolutionary impact on your life. This is the place where intuition can be found.

Furthermore, you may find the message strikes you as important because it comes across as very simple and direct. When we activate the right brain, it seems we are able to bypass some of the traditional left-brain functions. The right-brain functions are not specifically responsible for putting food on the table, a roof over our heads, and cash in our bank accounts as are associated with the more left-brain functions. The right brain seems more focused on the big-picture items, including our destiny, karma, and the lessons we need to learn while on this planet. So, when you get one of these messages from the right brain, give it serious consideration before dismissing it. The information you receive from writing with your nondominant hand will reveal how different each side of your brain is and the role each side plays.

You may want to temporarily conclude the process after you complete your nondominant writing. You can return to the process later in the day or the next day to reflect upon what you've written. The delay can offer a fresh perspective. The objective is to create an opening for the right brain to step into the ring and throw a punch, or in this case, record some thoughts or ideas without fear of reprisal by the left brain. This is the rare opportunity for the right brain to capture your attention because by activating it, you are allowing it to communicate with you.

Do not feel as if the thoughts you put into your

Thought Revolution Journal must come out in perfect prose or grammatical form. To do so limits you and the fun of discovery. This will lead you to stop making entries because you won't have enough time to "do it right." Of course, this message derives from your rational left brain, but it serves effectively as another roadblock to unlocking your truths.

Remember that the journey you're on meanders through the mazes of your mind. Even more complicated are labyrinths: they're full of obstructing walls and dead ends. In this process, you must give yourself permission to be spontaneous and sloppy, to backtrack and sniff out the hidden cracks in the barricades. From time to time, you may find yourself drawing a picture of the situation or making a diagram that lays out the relationships between aspects of an issue. Go with the flow. You're unfolding your own life to yourself. Once you've put something on paper, you can always come back to it and interpret its meaning, or use your nondominant hand to gain further insight and perspective.

As you chronicle the journey and note the nooks and crannies along the way, you travel toward more active understanding of your life's purpose and come alive to its possibilities. As strange as it sounds, the act of writing takes the expression out of your head. You can no longer deny its existence or let it float off into obscurity. The idea now has a tangible "shape," so you can't ignore its reality or pretend you've never noticed it.

You must trust that you can find your way no matter how lost or blind you may feel at any given moment. Once you've begun to unwind the thread through the maze of yourself, you can't go home until you've captured the beast—whatever it may be—and slain it. The *Thought Revolution Journal* contains your charts and maps. What's the worst that might happen when you embark on this journey? You mess up a few sheets of paper. But the best that might unfold? Unleashing the mighty scope of your *whole* mind.

The process of mapping my thoughts and reflections in my *Thought Revolution Journal* has awakened in me an intense curiosity about how this all works and what it helped me accomplish. My active and life-long interest in the mind's journey pushed me beyond the basic questions and provoked me to wonder if others could apply the technique as meaningfully as I have. Just how powerful is the three-pound organ that occupies the inside of our heads? Leonardo da Vinci could write with one hand at the same time he would draw with the other. Imagine what you or I might accomplish if we trained ourselves to use our whole minds! Let's give it a try!

FIVE

INJECTING
TRUTH SERUM

WE CARRY A LOT OF JUDGMENT about the word *lie*. We don't think much, however, about what it means within the context of ourselves. Everything you believe to be true about yourself, your life in its present form, and the expectations you have about your future could all be self-preservation in the form of "lies" imposed by the left brain.

A very striking example took place with the retired chief executive officer of a successful national corporation. His first response to the question "If you were an animal, what animal would you be?" was "Lab." When I asked why, he explained that he had owned more than a dozen Labrador retrievers in his life. But when he answered the question using his nondominant hand, he wrote "tiger." To the question "Why?" he replied, "I have no earthly idea . . . but that is the damnedest thing I've ever seen in my life."

A second test subject, the CEO of a successful private company, also first answered the question with "dog." When he used his nondominant hand, though, he answered "monkey." Asked which animal his wife would claim he's more like, he laughed and replied, "The monkey, of course." He went on to analyze, "To be honest, I swing from project to project and city to city much more in character with a monkey than a dog."

Of course, every person who participates in this exploration displays such a striking contrast between the dominant and nondominant hands' answers. Not everyone consciously considers himself to be virtually the stereotype of man's best friend on the outside only to discover that he has a man-eating or tree-swinging beast inside. In fact, some people who haven't achieved the level of success of these CEOs consciously construct themselves as the soaring raptor (an eagle or hawk) while inside, they're a pussycat.

FAMILIAR TERRITORY

I'm willing to bet that, at least once in a while, you've encountered your whole mind's capabilities. Think back to a momentous decision—whether to marry or buy a house, for instance. How did you arrive at the ultimate decision? If you're like me, you weighed options . . . and then you weighed them again. You might have felt pressure from others—your future spouse or your realtor—to make up your mind.

Rationally, you did everything you could to make certain your choice turned out for the best. But in the end, at that last moment when you made the commitment or didn't, was it your rationality or your instincts in control?

Most of us resort to emotion and intuition when we finally "make up our minds." The thinking rational or "conscious" left brain gives us consideration after consideration until we almost literally don't know which way to turn. Too many options and too much analysis lead as much to confusion as to resolution. But our consciousness excels at following the thread of an idea to its conclusion. Unfortunately, when it perceives the future as wide open, it must follow so many threads that they become knotted into a wad of yarn that it cannot untangle. That's when the right brain with its instinctive strengths comes to the rescue. It slices directly through the tangle and lands sure-footedly on the other side—your decision made and your signature on the contract.

"Make up your mind!" We don't talk about "making up" the thinking, feeling, or intuitive portions of the mind. When we employ this imperative, we speak of the mind as a whole and see that the decision ultimately must incorporate both parts; otherwise, the decision will not endure or serve us efficaciously. Have you ever made a decision when you had some nagging doubt in the back of your mind? When you were "of two minds" about it? How did that work out? It never goes very well for me.

THE SYMPTOMS OF SUPPRESSION

What happens when the subtle doubts emitted from the right brain have no voice? When they have never expressed themselves before? The questions bring us to the type of material that most concerns me in this book. Self-doubts. Second-guesses. Recriminations. Lies we tell ourselves so effectively that we can't even see them for what they are. We locked them away so long ago, we've no idea they're still down there—let alone that we might possess the key to their cells. In fact, our rational minds don't want them released; imagine the havoc they'd wreak!

Instead, our conscious and rational mind imprisons the "monsters" and fogs over their existence with adages—turns of phrase that obscure the hidden truth. In this way, one part of our mind "makes up" another part. When we construct a conscious self-image around nothing but the scantest evidence or the weakest perceptions, we literally construct the story of our lives without any regard for the truth. We imagine it. I don't want to belittle the imagination because it resides largely in the right mind alongside emotion and intuition. And like them, imagination can play a central role in uncovering deeper truths. Yet, to the extent that we fictionalize a self-concept, we make it untrue rather than true. We'll look more closely at some favorite ways others have done this in the next section of the book.

For now, let's consider how two-mindedness can

lead us astray. We've learned that the rational mind is no fan of chaos. When the right brain encounters disorder, confusion, or poor self-concepts, it can't shut them off, hide them away, and let some other part of the mind handle them. The conscious left brain prefers comfort, familiarity, and low-risk situations. And this side of the mind dominates most of our thoughts. Little surprise, then, how handily and compulsively it manufactures excuses or, as I call them, lies.

The rational mind lies to the right mind, and it assimilates the erroneous self-concept. At appropriate moments, the right mind feeds it back to the left mind and the poor self-image becomes a "reality" out of which the conscious mind must operate. Through intuitive writing, this feedback loop can be broken.

MEDIATION FOR THE MIND

You might think of "intuitive writing" as the mental equivalent of "good cop, bad cop." Allegedly, the old police routine is effective because the suspect allies himself with the "good cop" in opposition to the threats of violence or torture from the "bad cop." Just as police officers playing different roles can lead to learning the truth in an interrogation, anyone can employ intuitive writing to unlock the rational left brain's bad-cop-like domination of the consciousness. When we tap into both the rational and the creative minds, we can efficiently arrive at the truth that reveals itself when both "good" and "bad" cops work together.

Even better, anyone can accomplish this goal without leaving the interrogation chamber to find a second cop! We carry them both around in our heads all the time. Yet, this process may seem foreign because we usually think about the mind as a single entity. The idea that we can tap into two distinctive sides of the mind seems odd, because most of us don't do it very much. Just as many people's arm strength differs between the right and left, the power of the two sides of our minds varies. We're always "working out" with the conscious left brain, but if we want the right brain to get stronger, we've got to exercise it, too.

In contrast, "we become more and more like ourselves as we grow older." Turns out, neuroscience justifies this adage. Pathways the brain uses for processing thoughts become ingrained over time. As people recall a previous thought in later sessions, he or she becomes faster at processing the "routine." That's the good news—learning happens. The bad news, however, hits when highly trained minds attempt to "think outside the box."

When we learn and practice a subject or task ("the box"), our thought patterns grow so well traversed that—like the mouse running its maze—we find it difficult to risk a new thought path, much less come up with some revolutionary thinking. The metaphor "I'm in a rut" appears almost literally true when scientists trace the patterns of specific thoughts. This phenomenon may also explain why we grow increasingly resistant to change as we age. For most of us, it is far easier to stay on the path we already know, even when that path doesn't always lead us to the aforementioned cheese.

THE IRONY OF "THE BOX"

If you've never heard the corporate lingo, "We just have to think outside the box," I'd bet you've never attended a strategic planning session or organizational meeting. It's ironic how much we overuse this statement because those of us who are likeliest to hear or say it have typically lived and worked "inside the box" for decades. How are those same people going to find their way out? How likely are they to arrive at "the next best thing" by using the same tools, the same patterns, the same way of thinking as they've employed for years? Learning intuitive writing prevented me from malingering among the boxed-in group.

I've taken this process experimentally thus far into corporate America to determine if intuitive writing can serve as an important supplement to the highly regarded Strengths, Weaknesses, Opportunities, and Threats Analysis (SWOT), which has been the go-to methodology in strategic planning sessions since it came out of Stanford University fifty years ago.

Initial results are very promising. At minimum, strategic planning participants report they are indeed "thinking outside the box" with new and unconventional ideas and possibilities they've written down, courtesy of their right brains.

In *Steve Jobs,* the biography of Steve Jobs by Walter

Isaacson, Jobs is quoted as having claimed that "Intuition is a very powerful thing, more powerful than intellect in my opinion." Jobs continued to speak of the importance of learning how to quiet the mind, see things more clearly, and live in the present.

If we need to "get out of the box," find ways to better compete globally, and be more creative, then we certainly need to find revolutionary new ways to think differently than we have in the past.

MY STORY . . . CONTINUED

When I worked for the bank, I devoted time the night before a team strategy meeting to tapping both sides of my mind. For years I practiced Benjamin Franklin's "moral algebra," a form of decision mapping or "T" analysis—proposed by Franklin in 1772—in which

MORAL ALGEBRA: A BRIEF HISTORY

In 1772, Joseph Priestly wrote his wise friend Benjamin Franklin asking how to proceed in resolving a complex life decision. Franklin's counsel was to perform moral algebra to resolve the issue. He suggested Priestly take a piece of paper, divide it in half, and make an exhaustive list of pros and cons. Then, after a few days, come back to the list and cancel out pros and cons that seem of equal weight. What is left in the balance, Franklin claimed, is the best answer. Today, many refer to this process as a "T" analysis for the columns dividing pros and cons.

one lists pros on one side of the "T" and cons on the other. Throughout my adult life, I have applied this drill to almost any situation that required an outcome. Above the horizontal bar of the T, I stated the problem, declared the challenge, or asked the question.

To determine the solution, I carefully evaluated the columns and paid attention to the importance or "weight" of each item. I didn't simply add up how many items fell into each column. By balancing the two sides, I discovered where I needed to focus. Results may not have revealed themselves immediately, but when I worked on the factors that are out of balance, I made progress toward a solution.

An analysis using multiple factors with assigned weights certainly appealed to the left-brained banker in me, and I used this process many times throughout my career. Perhaps most importantly, we used a variation of this process to help select the best location for a new bank. When we were ready to add a new bank, there were usually multiple possibilities for the new location. Most of the time, it was not obvious which one might be best. Some had better visibility, while others were in faster growing markets. We used this process to assign weights to each of the factors. Then we were able to rank each potential location based on a range of variables and then multiply the rating by the weighting of each variable to get a number reflecting the context of the decision. Bottom line: we made better decisions when we began deploying this approach.

Having armed myself with a good amount of experience in writing with my nondominant hand, I decided to integrate intuitive writing into the more traditional technique of problem analysis. I wondered whether it might work in the business world as well as it did in my personal life.

Combining the T analysis with intuitive writing quickly became a vital assessment tool for me whenever I needed to reach major decisions in any sphere of my life. And you won't believe how easily! Now, when I have to make a decision, I complete a data dump of pros and cons into the T-analysis format, evaluate and weigh the factors, turn the page, and pose the following question to my right mind:

What factor(s) have I not yet fully considered in this decision process?

Placing the pen in my nondominant hand, the answers flow almost magically. Initially, this "magic" stunned me. Brand-new thoughts effortlessly dropped from my pen. I couldn't believe that so many different ideas would crop up out of the blue. Odder still, most of the new material didn't appear on the T analysis. It seemed as if an unexplored pathway was activated, leading to the recesses of my mind. And better yet, many of the new ideas were dead on. Adding in the intuitive writing answers helped me ignite my genius within (or at least a different part of me), which ultimately revolutionized my thought processes.

I learned over the course of a decade the power of

applying intuitive writing to a decision. There were several business decisions through the years that I reversed when my right brain result did not concur after completing my T analysis. Earlier in my career, I may have had some of these thoughts in the form of gut instincts, but I would have dismissed them.

One example that comes to mind was the decision to postpone our bank's expansion and entry into a new market—Kansas City. It was a complicated issue with some potentially big benefits and rewards, but also some large risks. My T analysis suggested a "Go" decision and others in the company also favored this path. When I posed the question "Is now the appropriate time for us to enter the Kansas City market?" I was stunned when my nondominant hand wrote, "No" in big letters. Further questions I posed and answered suggested the risks outweighed the benefits. We put the expansion "on hold." Months later, a windfall fell into our lap as we were able to make important hires mitigating much of the initial risk of failure in a new market.

The idea to write this book is the byproduct of a thought process about what I wanted to be intentional about doing with the rest of my life. Writing a book never registered on my bucket list before. It wasn't until I invoked the right-brain writing process did the notion of writing this book surface.

SIX

LET'S DRAW
A PICTURE

IS A PICTURE REALLY WORTH a thousand words? The answer is "yes," especially if you draw the picture. Sometimes pictures show an idea more readily than words, and, for some people, the most direct route to their creativity comes through drawing. I've employed drawing as part of my work with the nondominant hand for more than a dozen years. I find it particularly useful when I get stuck in my efforts to write out some part of the problem or possible solutions. When one wants simply to get something down on paper, drawing may yield more immediate results than writing.

Before we jump into an investigation of the lies we tell ourselves, let's take a moment to add the drawing skill to your repertoire of right-minded techniques. Imagine that this exercise will provide a baseline reading of your current life situation. Though it involves drawing, do not worry that anyone expects you to do what da Vinci could.

Get out your *Thought Revolution Journal,* a pencil, or a box of crayons, and on a blank page, write:

This is my life now.

Using your dominant hand, draw a picture that represents your response to this statement. Take a moment to consider what you've chosen to draw and why. After you've completed the first drawing, go to the next page, switch hands, take a big breath, clear your mind, reread the statement, and allow another drawing to take shape. Don't feel you must draw something typical or representational for either of these pictures. They may be abstract. That's fine. Next, compare the two drawings, which may be different from one another. At first, you might not know how to interpret the second drawing. Simply ask yourself:

What does the drawing represent?

Then, answer the question with your nondominant hand (using words this time). Often, this simple exercise brings up deep feelings and profound ideas. Be prepared. If that's what happens for you, rest assured that your reaction is a completely healthy and reasonable consequence of tapping into a portion of your mind with which you have not conversed in a long time.

When Nora, a successful businesswoman, agreed to participate in intuitive drawing, she drew a picture of her family with her nondominant hand. As we examined it, I noticed the figure she identified as her husband stood by itself on one side of the page. When

I pointed that out to her, Nora told me she didn't know why she had drawn her picture like that. So, I asked her to use that same hand to write about the "meaning" of the picture. When she did, she uncovered the insight "My husband is lonely."

On some level, Nora felt a distance between her husband and the rest of his family and thought it may have stemmed from some form of loneliness, but she had not become consciously aware of the situation until her right mind exposed it to her—first in a picture and then in words.

With that awareness she remarked, "I never really thought much about the fact that my husband might feel lonely. I really need to talk with him about that. I've been so immersed in my new business during the past year that I may have taken him for granted."

Simple and profound, simultaneous intuitive drawing and writing allows insights and answers to slip out of the subconscious and depict themselves on the page.

Like those with whom I've shared this technique, and each of the people you'll soon read about, I hope you gain some relief from whatever doubts and insecurities plague you. They no longer need to weigh you down. As you gain experience and practice drawing or writing the current state of your life or exploring your roadblocks, you'll become adept at spotting the lies you tell yourself. Before long, these excuses and lies will practically jump off the page. Then you can clear the way for the possibilities of achievement and realization of the true you.

Each of the following stories in the next part involves a real person and focuses on a common lie. I've been guilty of telling myself most of these at one time or another, so it wouldn't surprise me if you have too. Each story follows the main character through the encounter with his or her lie and the injection of some "Truth Serum" by means of intuitive writing. In each case, I've arranged the discussion to double as an exercise for you to take part in. Follow along as we resolve some of the most common lies we tell ourselves.

PART TWO

LIFTING
THE
EIGHT
LIES

SEVEN

LIBERATION
FROM LIES

ALL OF US HAVE CHINKS IN OUR ARMOR. Isn't it better to pretend they don't exist, to put some extra padding around the sore spots or throw up another wall-like defense? When a person is on her own battleground, isn't she in complete control of whether she triumphs or fails?

I recently talked an Oxford-educated economist into trying the animal exercise. Using his right hand, he answered "large cat." Then, he explained, "Well, something strong, you know, like a jaguar in the jungle." While I was still pondering the three syllables of his British pronunciation for "jag-u-ar," this sophisticated and well-dressed man's left hand answered the same question with "small house cat, like a Siamese." He continued to list the characteristics he shared with a house cat: "relaxation in any circumstance, independence, aloofness." As he finished writing down the third of these characteristics, he remarked, "Oh! I wasn't expecting that! It's dead on."

Had this well-educated, astute man fooled himself into thinking his approach to the world resembled a sleek, secretive predator more than a self-motivated, yet aloof Siamese? Not really. More likely he consciously aspires to present himself as a jaguar, but recognizes that, below the surface, most people see him as a strong-willed, well-bred, distant housecat. But a larger question arises: As long as factors like these remained unconscious to him, how clear a picture of his own playing field could this man have? Had he been fully honest with himself until he opened himself to the unexpected?

Consider the Truth Serum I provide for each of the eight lies that follow. At times, you may feel as if the shell has come off and left you defenseless. I assure you, though, that you can gain strength from exposing your lies through a process that may ultimately render your familiar shell obsolete. Once you hone your intuitive writing skills, it will become much easier to stay true to yourself because you will recognize yourself more fully in the revelations of each exercise. The lies and denials will diminish, and you might even send some of that old armor off to the museum.

A friend read an early draft of this book. "What did you think?" I asked her.

"Interesting," she replied.

"Did you do any of the exercises?"

"No, but I will."

Months passed. Every so often, I reminded her of her pledge to try the exercises. One day she agreed. We sat down at my kitchen table and I posed the question:

Am I lying to myself about anything?

Bingo! Over the course of the next hour and a half my friend discovered, as she put it, "I had been in total denial about certain aspects of my life for the last couple of years." Better yet, she began to identify why and proposed several ways of approaching the problem. She came up with such astonishing insights, in fact. I asked why she had put off trying these exercises for months. Her answer? "I suppose I just wasn't ready to learn the answer to that question."

To do any good, you must personally apply the principles from this book and unlock the gates to your whole mind. The beast at the middle of the maze doesn't need to come looking for you; it's perfectly comfortable devouring the endless supply of cheese where it dwells. Whether jaguar or pussycat, giant radioactive rat or little white lab mouse, you've got to go looking for it yourself. Sure, who isn't busy? If you're anything like me, you're probably an expert at rationalizing the lie "I don't have time."

It will very likely cause you some pain and effort to go back and do the work outlined. It will be worth your time. A more intentional, authentic, and happier life awaits you.

EIGHT

Lie Number 1
"EVERYTHING WILL WORK OUT EVENTUALLY," AKA "WHATEVER WILL BE WILL BE."

OFTEN WE ALLOW UNFORTUNATE CIRCUMSTANCES to prevail because we imagine that we will eventually figure out how to overcome them, or we pray the situation will work itself out. We don't expend much effort to work things through because, even if our current choices don't yield the best results, we probably won't be stuck with the present situation forever. Sooner or later something has to happen that will allow us to move on.

If the truth will eventually surface, why bother rushing it? As it turns out, being honest with oneself relates directly to living one's life to the fullest. If a person delays consideration of important issues and does not confront the lies she tells herself, then she has little hope of finding fulfillment. But if the person finds courage to take on his limitations and work to uncover the truth, he usually will lead a much more satisfying and rewarding life as a result.

MEET LAURA

When Laura learned that I was writing this book, she volunteered to be a test subject. In her mid-fifties and divorced, Laura hadn't dated for several years and indicated that she wasn't terribly happy with her life at the time.

For our first exercise, I suggested Laura use her nondominant hand to draw a picture of her life. After about five minutes, she showed me her drawing. To my eye, it depicted a child-like image of a house with many paned windows and the stick figure of a

Laura's nondominant hand response.

person standing to the left of the house. Next, I asked her to write with her nondominant hand the question, "What does the drawing mean?" Then, I had her switch hands again and answer the question.

Laura explained her drawing with these words: "My house is filled with all this stuff that I've bought as a substitute for having a relationship with a real person. No one can come inside my house because it's too full." As Laura wrote these words, she started to cry. I told her to just sit quietly for a few minutes.

After thinking about what she'd drawn and written, Laura confessed that she held on to all these possessions because she imagined they could protect her. She had become a hoarder, and the addiction had taken over her life. What I had mistaken for window-panes were actually piles of boxes inside her house. I know it's difficult to imagine someone I didn't know well would be willing to be so vulnerable by sharing her drawing. I've noticed when people get in the zone activated by the right brain, they are more able to stay focused in resolving the issue they are writing about.

"By nature," Laura said, "I used to be quite gregarious. I liked to throw parties and share my good fortune with friends. But sadly, no one except me has been inside my house for almost ten years."

A decade earlier, when her fiancée called off the wedding, Laura retreated from the world. I had her ask herself, "How did this happen?" She replied with her left hand, "You gave up on people. You put all your time and effort into beautiful things instead."

Rather than concentrate on the central issue in her life, Laura spent more time with her hobby of collecting and reselling antiques. She became so obsessed, in fact, that she couldn't sell things as fast as she bought them. They piled up inside her house until they closed out the possibility of a primary love relationship and ties with friends and acquaintances.

Laura had fallen into a self-destructive pattern. Though she basically knew she didn't feel happy, she hadn't given it much thought. She persisted with binge-like purchases to make her feel a little better. She ignored the boxes in her house because she told herself she could sell the things eventually. In effect, she had convinced herself that everything would work out eventually. But that wasn't the truth.

Seldom does divine intervention, or magic, play a role in uncovering the truth. Yet, we often act as though the truth is more easily denied than dealt with. Laura must have figured that, in time, she would find her way out of the hoarding problem and begin again to entertain and to date. Yet, instead of confronting head on either the lie or the truth, she told herself she had better things to do.

Why did this smart, usually sensible woman put so much effort into piling up a wealth of beautiful things just so she could ignore the poverty of her relationships? Did some part of her imagine that her addictive behavior was her best—or only—choice? Was she waiting for something to happen that would break her out of her funk? Is that why she quickly volunteered to try the nondominant handwriting exercise? Until Laura took that step she hadn't given much thought to her own best interests. Or maybe it took those ten years and the piles of antiques to force her to face the truth.

What goes on in the mind when we think about our difficulties? Often, the nurturing mind puts a little salve on the wound and we get on with our business. The rational side of the mind hopes to avoid conflict, pain, or any disruption of the status quo. It simply embraces the notion that there's no need to enter into the battle of figuring out our truths today. Laura found it easy to remain in denial because she believed her problems would work themselves out eventually.

She didn't take action because she thought that somehow the universe would come to her rescue. Her rational thinking mind convinced the intuitive and emotive mind to stand down because it argued, "The truth will eventually surface." Her intuitive side didn't feel completely closed off from the "decision," since there was a prospect for the truth to surface in time. In fact, given the creative mind's greater connectedness to intuition, Laura readily believed her own lie.

Laura believed that the truth behind her behaviors —both her hoarding and her avoiding love—would surface on its own. Rather than put any effort into action that might resolve these problems, Laura spent the best part of ten years "copping out" because she didn't think she had any responsibility to seek the truth. It would find her when it was ready. And, in one way, she was right. The truth eventually revealed itself, but with wasted years of isolation and pain. When she finally listened to the needs of her unconscious right brain, Laura learned how to get out of delay mode and focus on what she needed to confront.

TRUTH SERUM, DOSE 1:
"Can the truth set me free?"

The extent to which we tackle our issues, limitations, and problems directly relates to the progress we make in our lives. If you fail to find your uniqueness, or if you're not true to yourself, such self-betrayal can become a tragic flaw.

On the subject of truth, we have two adages: "Truth hurts" and "The truth can set you free." Whether or not it hurts to learn the truth, denying it certainly can inflict huge tolls on you . . . and on those around you. It did exactly that for Laura. Perhaps, then, the freedom that comes from knowing the truth is little more than freedom from the emotional strain of trying to deny it.

As we've seen, the hurtfulness of this lie compounds when the liar abdicates personal responsibility. Laura told herself that she didn't have to focus on the issue immediately because she believed that "the truth will eventually surface." Such thinking let Laura off the hook because, through it, she avoided looking more deeply at herself. But what happened when she started to look below the surface after more than ten years?

Once Laura recognized and admitted the damaging influence of her hoarding, she continued exploring the possibilities this admission afforded her. I suggested she write down the question:

Since I feel so miserable now, should I make some changes in my life?

What happened next completely amazed us both. Her composure restored, Laura calmly used her left hand to put on paper a nine-point plan that could help her progress beyond the pain and obstructions she'd instilled in her life.

Almost as if her creative mind had simply waited for this opportunity to present the solutions, Laura stared at her words in disbelief. Halfway begrudgingly, she told me, "Why couldn't I have figured this out ten years ago? It makes so much sense, and there's really nothing stopping me from doing it!"

Over the next seven months, Laura dutifully followed her plan for freedom. At the end of that time she invited a relative to visit and hosted a small party at her house to celebrate the occasion. I watched in amazement as a gregarious, warm, and sociable person came back to life. With nothing more than an hour of using her nondominant hand and some determination, Laura resolved the problem she had wrestled with for ten years.

My appreciation for the complexity and directness of the human mind grew from witnessing Laura's progress. The bad habit that trapped her for ten years practically went up in smoke when I gave her the opportunity to tap into her creative mind. She not only gained the insight that she needed to change, she realized exactly how she could go about it.

If Laura's friends or family members had made the same suggestions she discovered through intuitive writing, I believe that she probably wouldn't have followed their solutions. Instead, Laura may have felt judged and become defensive, and thus, more resistant to making the changes she needed. It was because Laura identified the issues on her own terms and experienced her own "Aha!" moment, that she could proceed confidently to a resolution.

If you believe you're telling yourself the lie "Everything will work out eventually," inject some of the same truth serum Laura used by asking:

What am I not honest with myself about?

Write this question in your *Thought Revolution Journal*. Then use your nondominant hand to answer the question. If you draw a blank, try asking:

Is there something or someone in my life I avoid?

You can follow these questions with:

Why can't I be honest about X? Or why can't I face X?

Switch hands back and forth to let your dominant hand write the questions and your nondominant answer. Your objective is to become a detective and discover whether you are in denial of an essential truth about yourself and the manner in which you keep it hidden.

Ultimately, tapping into your whole mind has the great value of helping you discover what you already know but don't perceive as the "rational" answer. The easier course of resisting change and avoiding pain usually doesn't yield positive results, but still we cling to it as Laura did because we know we don't like pain. By allowing the creative right mind's resources to slip past the guardhouse of our logical left mind, we can explore the labyrinth of options our whole mind presents.

NINE

LIE NUMBER 2
"I'LL GET TO IT LATER."

SINCE WE LIVE IN A BUSY and harried world, we are too preoccupied to attempt something complicated, and so we end up postponing it. For a couple days we can get away with putting off a simple task, such as taking out the garbage. But what about those big goals? How do we discern a benign procrastination from a harmful avoidance tactic (lie) put in place by our left brain? For the most part, the lie that "there's always time to get to it later" enables procrastination. Whether the thing we put off is fun or work, a diet or exercise regimen, or making a difficult phone call, our early training allows us to think it is okay to postpone.

We delude ourselves with the notion that time is infinite. When someone takes that thinking to an extreme, she or he becomes a chronic procrastinator believing any assignment will eventually be completed and never imagining an urgent need to work on a project before the due date. "I am better under pressure," is another common version of Lie Number 2. In some cases, people who adopt this mantra probably don't relish the task in the first place. In others, one side of the mind may object to the job or subconsciously feel inadequate about the ability to perform it. But chronic procrastinators become so habituated to putting things off that they hardly need an excuse from either side of the mind. It simply feels comfortable and right for them to postpone things. "That's just who I am. It's my M.O.," they justify.

We are all creatures of habit. We reinforce both good and bad habits indiscriminately. We do so because our thinking minds prefer routine and embrace regularity. Breaking a habit can be possible, but it's difficult. First the person must break through the barrier of the long-held pattern before he or she can find a new pattern and begin implementing it as familiar behavior.

The habit of procrastination takes root deep in the psyche. Certainly it may make sense to delay the occasional project for valid reasons, but delay for the sake of delaying makes no logical sense at all. Procrastinators often postpone action in lieu of other "responsibilities," such as cleaning house, returning phone calls, spending some time with the kids, or taking advantage of the great weather.

They give these excuses, by the way, whether or not they actually engage in them. Whatever the favorite excuse, almost everyone falls victim to procrastination from time to time.

MEET SAM

When he was a teenager, Sam struggled with being overweight and out of shape. Once he got to college, he maintained a normal weight and fitness level by staying reasonably active, but when he entered the workforce as assistant manager of a grocery store, Sam's job kept him on his feet all day. At the end of the day, his feet hurt from walking on uncarpeted cement floors. Now thirty, his back ached most days, too.

Though he knew better, Sam often skipped breakfast and snacked throughout the day rather than taking time to sit down and eat. He looked forward to the end of the day when he could go home and relax, which equated to picking up fast food, watching TV, and having a couple beers after dinner. He always intended to get back in shape. He even made resolutions about exercising like he'd done in college, but he never stuck to any of these plans for more than a week or two.

What was "wrong" with Sam? Simply put, he became victim to one of the most common lies of all. Sam could never wrap his mind around the concept that the only "right" time is right now. He really had only two choices: stay in his rut and continue to live in slowly deteriorating health or change his nutrition and start moving.

The six words "I can always do it later" seem so harmless, almost prudent—even responsible. What's wrong with postponing something in order to get something in front of us accomplished?

When Sam was a boy and anticipated something fun, Sam's mom often told him "Now, let's not rush into anything. We need to plan for that." When he wanted his father to play catch with him, he often heard, "Daddy's too tired right now. Maybe later." When he asked to join the fencing and archery teams in high school, the equipment cost too much. When he wanted to go on a camping trip with a friend, he first had to clean his room and mow the lawn to earn the privilege. When he planned to bike to the creek and take his granddad's old rod and reel, he heard the familiar refrain from his mom or dad, "You can do that later. First you need to . . ."

Such parental rationales and supposed reasonable delays seem to make sense because they imply greater fun and productivity happen as a result of putting play before work. But in Sam's case, they also taught him to neglect pleasant physical activity for the benefit of work. In fact, that idea became so firmly implanted in him that it now obstructed him from any progress toward becoming more physically fit and healthier.

Sam's childhood programmed him to accept delay until a "more appropriate" moment in the future. The left side of his mind—and to a large extent, the right side, too—accepted waiting for enjoyment as a simple fact of life. Not surprisingly, however, the creative mind craves activity that opens new vistas and expands possibilities.

All the time, a tug-of-war was taking place in Sam's mind.

The intuitive part proposed that he have some fun in an activity that would stimulate his body and raise his heart rate. The more rational side said, "Okay, but you really don't feel like it right now, do you? Pay attention to your aching back and feet. What are they going to feel like when you stress them more with exercise?" The creative mind suggests, "Let's figure it out together." It calls on the argumentative mind to develop a "reasonable" plan. But all too often, the logical mind has virtually given up on what it sees as a hopeless attempt to persuade "the authorities" when almost every past attempt has required some sort of "payment" before the fun can start.

The pragmatic-thinking left mind overpowers the message from the creative right mind, gives in to history, and postpones the fun—no matter how much good it might do for the whole mind, body, and even soul. The mental tug-of-war takes place so quickly that the person inside is unaware, for the most part, of what is transpiring in his or her own head.

How many times did you succeed at getting your parents to let you visit your friend next door before you had done your homework, cleaned your room, or completed whatever task you were given? No matter how much the right mind may crave fun and games, it doesn't have the power to persuade parents, teachers, or bosses to change their minds.

Parents rarely tell their children, "I'm sure there'll

be time for you to do your homework later." Maybe they ought to. Perhaps only a few children are diligent enough on their own to play now and work later. But if Sam's parents had relented once in a while and allowed him to be a bit more of a child, maybe he wouldn't have found himself in a debilitating situation later in life. He learned so well to postpone fun that he couldn't find the energy to do otherwise.

TRUTH SERUM, DOSE 2:
"If I wait too long, it might never get done."

When Sam got home one evening, he decided to practice the intuitive writing he had learned from his friend earlier in the day. He used his dominant right hand to ask, "Why do I put up with always feeling bad?" With his left hand his inner voice answered, "You treat your dog better than you treat yourself. You don't overfeed him. Get help, read, and learn what you need to know to take care of yourself." On Monday, Sam called employee assistance and inquired whether the company's insurance program would provide a health coach. It did. And Sam followed through.

At last, Sam took a step that could lead to better health and an improved life. To overcome Lie Number 2, you must first distinguish those things you legitimately want to delay from those you would rather deny, ignore, or never do at all.

But what if Sam had gone on waiting to make that decision? Would he have gotten healthier without taking some step that led to physical activity and better eating habits? Not very likely. When it comes to exercise, the conundrum is that you've got to do it for it to have any effect. Avoid it and you'll wind up dead . . . and probably much sooner than you might have if you'd gotten off your backside.

If you think you live under the influence of "There's always time to do it later," consider giving yourself an injection of the same truth serum Sam took: "If I wait too long, it might never get done." In this case, Sam literally could have risked the longevity of his life, solidifying the fact that time is not to be squandered.

Get out your *Thought Revolution Journal*. Pose a question about your procrastination. Are you putting something off? What is it? To "road test" the technique, start with a task (big or small) you know you routinely delay or object to performing. Use your dominant hand to ask:

Why do I let myself think that there's always time to do X later?

Now, switch the pen to your nondominant hand and write the answer to the question. Eventually, if procrastination is one of your faults (as it is for many of us), you can drill deeper by asking the following questions:

Do I have a good reason to postpone this task?
If so, what is it?
If not, what's keeps me from getting started?

When you've gotten your answers, you can always

come back to the *Thought Revolution Journal* later in order to analyze your responses and consider their implications. Very likely you will gain some insights that you didn't have before. Or you may find—if you are completely honest with yourself—that your answers merely reveal exactly what you already sensed was true. Either way, if you act on the revelation, you'll ultimately become happier and more confident.

TEN

LIE NUMBER 3
"SOONER OR LATER MY SHIP WILL COME IN," AKA "GOOD THINGS COME TO THOSE WHO WAIT."

MUCH LIKE THE TWO PRECEDING LIES, our sense of time is the culprit as we wait for our "ship to come in." Rather than accept the status of our lives, we want to believe things will *eventually* "turn around" and work out the way we dreamed. We justify this next lie on the pretense that time will never come to an end and imagine that, with a little faith, everything will work out in our self-interest. But the keyword is "eventually." Accepting the endless extension of time implied in that word lulls us into a false sense of comfort. Then we become complacent and make no progress at all. Since we believe we have plenty of time, we feel no need to accomplish our goals now. The antidote to this lie is for us to honor our current life circumstances, even if they don't remotely resemble where we want to end up; then we can take some action.

MEET JACKIE

Though she was twenty-seven, Jackie toiled six days a week for a company that paid her little and gave her joyless menial tasks. She had a degree in psychology, but it wasn't getting her anywhere. Jackie talked about returning to school to become a physical therapist, but she didn't earn enough money to afford full-time tuition.

Jackie felt trapped and longed for satisfying work and the rewards of a more lucrative career. Together, Jackie and I worked through a few simple questions, beginning with:

Why do I feel conflicted about doing what I know I should?

With her nondominant hand, she wrote, "You are so afraid of making a mistake it is paralyzing you."

Why had Jackie not noticed this paralysis before this moment? Because her attention had been focused elsewhere. I believe Jackie imagined that some universal "justice" would one day play out and bring her the proverbial happy ending to her life's story. After all, she knew she deserved it; she had always led an honest and productive life. But a potential trap lurks inside the thought that "one day my ship will come in." Rather than taking action and shaping her own life, Jackie gave herself permission to stay where she was, despite her misery. Because she believed she would *eventually* get what she wanted, she had no reason to address—or pay attention to—her current condition.

For years, Jackie kept telling herself that the time wasn't right for a change. If she just kept plugging away at the job she hated, maybe she'd eventually pull together enough resources to enable her to break free and return to school. Meanwhile, Jackie ignored the fact that "time was a wasting" and perhaps her ship would never arrive if she did nothing about waving it in.

Before we got to the question that finally allowed Jackie to recognize her paralysis, I had her ask:

When am I going to study physical therapy?

Her nondominant hand spelled out "L-a-t-e-r." I inquired what she thought she meant by that, and she said to me, defensively, "It's going to happen! There's plenty of time for things to change." So, I asked her to respond to the question, "Is there something that needs to change before I can go back to school?" Jackie said, "I have to get everything ready first." But what did she really need to prepare other than her frame of mind? When Jackie wrote "L-a-t-e-r," she instantly realized that rather than "sooner or later," she actually believed "*later*, her ship would come in." This was a turning point for her.

How do we discriminate whether our reasons can justify postponement? If we don't line up the necessary information, tools, resources, or people, it's premature to begin a task. Postponing is appropriate if everything isn't in place, if proper preparation has not been done.

On the other hand, we delay inappropriately when we choose not to proceed despite the fact that everything we need is ready. In the latter case, we typically fashion an excuse that revolves around one of two lies: "There's always time to do it later" or "Someday my ship will come in."

Perhaps it would help to turn the metaphor of the ship around a little. What if Jackie thought of herself as the ship sailing on the ocean? In high school and college, she excelled at her studies without working all that hard. In that way, her ship set sail on smooth seas. But now that she was dissatisfied with her job, the ship had run into a squall. Jackie thought someone on the bridge was studying the charts and steering to ensure

This is my life now...

Jackie's nondominant hand response.

the ship could weather the storm and arrive in port without too great a delay. Jackie didn't feel terribly concerned since the ship obviously hadn't taken on water or run out of fuel.

Jackie had yet to discover an alarming truth: the bridge was empty! On the ship of your life, you must serve as passenger, captain, and crew. As this fact began to dawn on Jackie, she grew uncertain about how her boat would make it to port. Sailing without maps, radar, and a pilot isn't very wise, but that's essentially what Jackie had been doing for close to five years.

Two pieces of folk wisdom influenced Jackie's complacency and reluctance to take charge of her life. She believed "good things come to those who wait" and that she should "just sit back and enjoy the ride." Though many of us are forced to learn long-suffering patience, to expect that patience alone can correct the course of a ship blown astray by a squall is a mistake. And while it makes sense to relax and appreciate a pleasure cruise, few of us would want to sail for years without reaching some destination.

Convincing ourselves that we have no need to confront today's problems is a sure-fire way to prolong them. How many times do we allow ourselves to postpone an important discussion or fail to follow through on a resolution because we believe that "things will work out the way they're supposed to"? We are certain that better days are ahead.

Absolutely nothing is wrong with any of these concepts. We should enjoy individual moments in life. We should relax and let some things unfold in their own way and time. Patience is a virtue when applied appropriately. And sometimes things *do* work themselves out. Yet, when the moments of waiting turn into days, days into weeks, weeks into years, can anyone honestly say that she is happy waiting for the ship to come? Jackie couldn't.

From time to time, the wise pilot steers a course for change. Yes, almost everyone finds change risky because it's so much easier to stick with what we know—even if it's not in our best interest. While we're hanging around the port, we tell ourselves "our ship will come in sooner or later." But we don't realize that we are the masters of our own destiny, possessing the ability to steer our own ship, sail with it to its destination, and set the sails and trim the sheets all by ourselves. Though we may not want to "rock the boat," we'll never get anywhere if we don't set sail.

In extending our metaphor even further, the rational mind prefers to sail on smooth seas—even though it may not know the final destination. It contents itself to sail over familiar waters and let the rest of the mind worry about the rough seas that will come inevitably. Because the ship survived storms in the past, the linear mind confidently assumes that it can keep the boat from capsizing if another storm comes along.

For the most part, the rational mind does not care to consider other ports or destinations than the one it has fixed its course for. Jackie allowed her thinking mind to steer for predetermined destinations despite her intuitive sense to head somewhere else. Why? Because to some extent she believed the lie "I don't need to rush." She imagined that she had "all the time in the world" to get where she was going and saw no reason to head in another direction based on a hunch. And, by the way, if she stuck to her course, the bigger and better ship that held her true destiny would never have sailed into port.

TRUTH SERUM, DOSE 3:
"Will I get what I need if I wait long enough?"

As we sail along on the ship of our own lives, we leave our home ports far behind. We won't be there when "our ship comes in," because our lives have moved inexorably onward while we thought we were standing around waiting. Believing that "sooner or later my ship will come in" implies that patience always brings the reward. That could happen, but it doesn't very often.

How could Jackie distinguish between a healthy sense of patience and the lie she entertained? Almost all of us learn early on that activities have their proper time and place. The healthy side of this lesson teaches us patience. Like Sam, Jackie learned as a child that it's best to take one's time to complete homework, play games, plan vacations, enjoy the moment, or reach for one's dreams. Jackie's nondominant hand response "later" helped her to understand she was in a trap. She subscribed to the belief she did not have to take any immediate action because "good things come to those who wait." She realized she was postponing the decision-making process and would continue doing so until she realized the pattern. When she learned she was puttin off even *thinking* about going back to school, she knew she had to "snap out of it." No one else would ever be able to resolve the trap she was in. She was the one who would have to go back to school—nobody could do it for her.

There was potentially never going to be a good time to go back to school, and after more nondominant handwriting and introspection, Jackie learned she had to take action now, rather than later; bite the bullet and get on with the life and career she wanted. Her dilemma was resolved by taking out student loans to go back to school and pursue the education she needed to become a physical therapist.

Take out your *Thought Revolution Journal.* With your dominant hand pose the question:

Why do I feel that I'm not getting what I need right now?

Then, use your nondominant hand to answer it. Next, write and answer the question:

What needs to change?

Finally, explore:

If I stay on my current path, where will I end up?

Expect bold answers, which you may choose to investigate further to learn as much as you can from the whole-mind perspective. Think of the exercise as a conversation with yourself, allowing you to probe your intuitive mind with the tough questions that may have gone unasked and unanswered for years. Like Jackie and Sam, you can stop procrastinating and postponing. Through this intuitive-writing exercise, you can learn how to reduce confusion about your aspirations and gain greater clarity about your personal needs and desires. The short answer to the question, "Will I get what I need if I just wait long enough?" is clear. No, you won't.

ELEVEN

LIE NUMBER 4
"I'M NOT THE ONE WHO NEEDS TO APOLOGIZE."

WHO LIKES TO ADMIT WHEN THEY'RE WRONG? We all make mistakes, yet owning up to them can be one of the most challenging things we do. We often think, *If the other person won't admit their wrongdoing, why should I?* Certainly, the lesson we learn these days from politicians, sports stars, actors, and televangelists teaches that one almost never apologizes unless caught red-handed. In fact, because of this socialization, we typically depict anyone who must make the big *mea culpa* as weak, ignorant, or complete losers. In today's fast-paced, technology-driven society, anyone can go from superstar to villain in an instant—especially when having to publicly own up to a mistake or error in judgment. With so much at stake, it's no wonder we feel the need to share the blame.

Nobody wants to "go down" alone, so self-preservation takes over. Sincere apologies, of course, should be just the opposite. An honest apology sets the record straight. If we fail to apologize when we should—particularly if we do so because we imagine the other person should say he or she is sorry as well—we're pretending that everything's okay when we know it isn't. We lie to ourselves yet again. If I start with the assumption "I'm always the one to apologize," my expression of regret holds little sincerity; I'm just doing it because someone must.

We often act as if we've got an imaginary scorecard somewhere inside our heads. We use it to track our daily interactions: "Score two points for me, one for her." In particular, we track big wins and losses: "I believe I'm up four games to two." Our internal scorecard helps us determine winners and losers, and no one wants to lose. When we become really good at "knowing the score," we can move on to track statistics, too. In this way, life becomes more about competition than honor. Too many times, we accept that winning is the game. We learn it in little league and in movies. We pursue it at work and in academia. Little wonder it leaks into our relationships with friends, family, coworkers, and companions.

For me, the belief that "I don't need to apologize" grows out of my focus on winning. To the extent I believe this lie, I do so because I accept the notion that I want to "win." As long as I feel justified in my quest to do what I must to win, I'm not very likely to apologize for potentially hurtful acts. Perhaps I should confess that I'm not especially proud of this trait, but it has certainly helped me climb the ladder of success.

Do you think apologizing diminishes your power and the way people perceive you? Would you rather get away with running a red light or telling a white lie than paying the consequences or apologizing? You rationalize that you'll "apologize" if you're caught. This is because your logical mind has an interest in maintaining the status quo. None of us rationally plans to threaten his livelihood, well-being, family, or position of power. From the outlook of protecting our personal interests, the left mind dominates internal discussions and decision-making about when and under what conditions to apologize.

But in the spirit of competitiveness and ego-based living, what are we costing ourselves and each other? I've seen colleagues sabotage each other to get a promotion, friends stop talking over petty things, and family members hold grudges over something said ten Thanksgivings ago—all in the name of "being right." But what we will see in the following story is the disservice we are doing ourselves and the person whom we believe owes us an apology. Too many times within these imprudent excuses innocent people get dragged into the drama and wind up suffering as well.

MEET SALLY

A working single mother by choice, Sally often felt pulled in many directions. She wouldn't complain, though, because she'd wanted her daughter so much.

After deciding she couldn't wait any longer to become a mom, Sally received artificial insemination. Almost five weeks before her thirty-second birthday, Sally received the best present anyone could want—a healthy baby girl whom she named Rebecca.

As junior partner in a law firm, Sally had the financial footing for day care. While she had the monetary and educational responsibilities of parenthood planned out, receiving emotional support was a bit trickier. Sally wished she could count more on her mother to pick up some of the slack that comes with being a single mom, but she hadn't quite forgiven her mother for the unsupportive reaction she received after delivering the news that she was pregnant.

According to her mother, Sally had no business having a child on her own, so Sally seldom took Rebecca to visit her grandmother. Sally did want Rebecca to have the same close relationship with her grandmother that Sally had enjoyed with hers. Sally knew that would be an impossibility unless the rift between her and her mom was repaired. With several years already spent harboring resentment, Sally didn't know how to mend the relationship after all this time.

In Sally's case, some of her stubbornness stemmed from her own competitive nature. No one becomes partner in a law firm of any size at twenty-eight without a fair amount of aggressive action. Sally's mother stopped teaching when her husband became a legal partner and she was pregnant with Sally. His long hours and social obligations regularly competed with her expectation that he should be a more active father. However, Sally's mom never managed to win that argument with her husband.

Then one day, Sally's dad died suddenly from a massive heart attack while at the office. He was only fifty-eight, and Sally's mom had to live with the fact that she hadn't told him goodbye that morning because they'd had a tiff over breakfast about whether he could afford time off to attend their younger son's hooding ceremony on the West Coast.

Sally recognized that her mom was doing her best to cope with her father's unexpected death. At the same time, she rejected that she had done anything wrong by wanting to become a mother herself. Sally was aware that her dad's death was one of the catalysts of wanting to have a child of her own.

Of course, she hadn't told her mother about these feelings because her mom's negative attitude had stung. Didn't she know that Sally had learned as much from her about being a parent as she had from her dad about being a lawyer? Just after Rebecca's first birthday, Sally's mom told her that she'd like to spend more time with the baby. She proposed watching Rebecca a couple of days each week. That would mean rescheduling with the day-care center, so Sally said, "That's okay, Mom. Becca and I are doing fine the way things are."

Do you think Sally is telling the truth?

TRUTH SERUM, DOSE 4:
"What might happen if I apologize?"

With the hope of some reconciliation in the back of her mind, Sally met up with her mom at their church's annual women's retreat Two things happened on that retreat that led Sally to reconsider her decisions about not apologizing to her mom and about letting her take care of Rebecca more often. During the first evening session when everyone was telling a little something about their lives, Sally's mother spoke of her ongoing sadness about the loss of her husband. Then, she told the group that she was delighted about her first grandchild and hoped Sally would let her play a bigger role in Rebecca's life than she had so far.

The next morning, one of the retreat leaders taught the participants about writing with their nondominant hand to gain insight into tough questions. With her mother's wishful words from the night before still in her ears, Sally used the quiet time to reflect more deeply on her relationship with her mom. In response to the question, "What happened to the special relationship Mom and I used to have?" Sally wrote with her left hand, "You judged her. It hurt. Tell her."

Later that day, Sally did just that. She and her mom walked in the garden and Sally told her she was sorry for not having been more available since her father's death. She expressed happiness that her mom wanted to spend more time with Rebecca and reminisced about time she'd spent with her mother's mother, after whom she had named her daughter. With tears in her eyes, Sally's mom expressed deep regret that she'd ever said anything negative about her pregnancy, and the two of them agreed that Grandma would watch Rebecca on Tuesdays and Thursdays.

What changed? First, Sally resolved to put aside her competitive feelings about whether she could be as good a mom as hers had been. Next, she decided to tell her mother how much it had hurt to hear her so flatly doubt Sally's commitment to her baby. Then she confessed her own feelings about her father's death before asking her mom to forgive her for the judgment Sally showed her during the period of her grief. As is so often the case when one apology is freely given, Sally's mother turned it around by admitting her own mistakes in choosing her words so poorly and for letting her grief affect her daughter.

When you make an apology that you know in your heart is necessary and proper, it becomes a mark of self-confidence. In Sally's case, when her nondominant hand spoke to her about her mother, she discovered a truth. With the statement "You judged her," Sally understood that both she and her mother had acted judgmentally. That revelation surprised Sally because up to that point her conscious mind led her to believe her mother had been the only one placing judgment. The insight showed her the two-sided nature of every relationship and gave her the resolve to apologize, whether her mother responded in kind or not. In the end, all it took was an apology to heal and progress their relationship.

Serving as moral compass, the intuitive mind comprehends the need to apologize much better than the logical mind. While both sides of the mind probably work together to distinguish right from wrong, we trust "logical" conclusions more than intuitions. But still, we feel regret from time to time. We foster competition and the desire to come out on top more vigorously in our linear thought. After all, what besides winning is the point of any game? It takes a lot of input from the intuitive mind to overcome the rational mind's reluctance to admit error or realize the need to apologize.

Like our minds, every apology has two sides. The "internal apology" happens when I admit to myself that I've committed some offense. At this juncture, the two sides of the mind communicate back and forth between themselves. You might see it as the linear mind apologizing to the intuition for not paying more attention to it and for condoning the misbehavior. Then, and only then, can I move on to make a sincere "external apology" to the person or persons I have wronged.

Under such circumstances, the act of apologizing liberates me from the bonds of negativity I've lugged around. By setting the record straight that the blame for such and such belongs to me, I balance myself. My sense of power and entitlement evens itself out to a more fitting one of self-esteem.

I don't want to lose touch with the proper humility or disconnect from those around me. Apologizing realigns the rational and intuitive minds. Too much disjunction between motive and behavior causes a schism in my head. I recognize the split when my anxieties or feelings of ill-ease peak shortly after a potentially questionable behavior. My mental state won't settle, and I give others the impression that I'm "out of sorts" or grumpy.

Reason protects the self-image. Effectively, it acts as a shield casting off dangerous missiles and absorbing blows. Its primary function is to keep us putting one foot in front of the other following the rational properties of time, manner, and place. In this way, it creates for us a self-identity that we can distinguish from any other. We believe ourselves to be single, unique individuals only because our rational minds tell us it's so. You can well imagine how first-rate the logical mind becomes at its task after decades of practice!

For someone who needs to make an apology, the obvious question arises: "How do I pierce the armor with which the rational brain protects my image of myself?" As you've probably realized by now, the process is fairly straightforward. The trick comes when you ask the rational mind to pay attention to its intuitive counterpart.

Modern culture always sides with reason over intuition, and where do you suppose modern culture is born? The subject must honor the whole mind rather than prefer one side to the other. To do so, most people must first build on the strengths of their creative minds. To get it to nurture me, I've first got to nourish it with experiences it can absorb and take part in. When we bypass the usual defenses of the rational mind by writing with our nondominant hands, we cock the trigger and shoot the silver bullet directly through the armor around our egos.

You'll need your *Thought Revolution Journal* again. If you're not currently troubled by an obvious occasion for apology, begin with the question:

Do I have something to regret or apologize for?

Allow your nondominant hand to respond with whatever comes to mind. When you have honestly completed just this much of the exercise, you will likely have a sense of relief. You will feel lighter, as if a weight has been lifted from you. Once you have your regrets in black and white, you can begin to think about what you've written and your action's consequences for others. If the list includes actions or behaviors of which you are not particularly proud, try not to be too hard on yourself. All of us make mistakes.

When you're ready to move on, pose the question:

What should I do about X?

Use your nondominant hand to answer this question for each item on your list. In determining the appropriate course of action, you may need to ask yourself who you might have hurt or mistreated. Or you may find that an apology is no longer appropriate because the object of your misbehavior has died or is otherwise no longer in your life. If you find yourself resistant to the thought of apologizing or making some other reparation, try the question:

If I do not apologize to X, will that make me happy? Will it make things right?

In any case, be certain to arrive at a definite course of action to follow through for each of the regrets in your list.

Tapping your intuitive brain helps you become honest, and the more honest you are with yourself and your plan of action, the more liberated you will feel— especially after you make your apologies or complete your reparations.

TWELVE

Lie Number 5
"MY LIFE IS AS GOOD AS IT GETS."

I MET ALBERT ON A PLANE from San Francisco to Hong Kong. He was on his way home to visit his parents; I would tour Indochina. In almost no time, I realized that I was sitting next to, and conversing with, one of the smartest people I'd ever meet. Within the year, Albert would graduate at the top of his class from one of the most prestigious medical schools in the United States. I assumed this guy must be on top of the world.

At various points in my life, people have thought that about me. Objectively, I recognize that my outward projections of my work, social, and public lives, could lead someone looking from the outside in to believe I have nothing to complain about. But what people didn't know that while I was sporting a fancy title on prestigious business cards and earning the financial wealth to afford almost any material item I desired, much of my life felt unsettled and I wondered for years what I lacked.

In my thirties, I finally realized that I had trouble accepting intimacy in relationships and therefore began to feel the isolation that a dedicated work life brought me. While I didn't avoid meeting new people, I could not get past a certain point with them. Once we'd gotten through the initial surface "getting to know one another" phase, the faster and harder I wanted to get out of there. It took me years to admit this difficulty, and I still face it at times.

Because I am an expert at almost all of the lies in this book, I rationalized that I had not met the right person yet. In other words, I kept waiting for "my ship to come in." By my mid-thirties, I had more or less accepted that it was okay not to be in a long-term relationship. So I stopped imagining that the "ship of love" would one day find me and invoked the lie "My life is as good as it gets." I should be happy with all the advantages and perks of a good job, a supportive family, lots of friends, etc., etc. But deep inside me, a flame of unhappiness consumed a lot of my spirit.

After a couple hours of talking to Albert, I glimpsed a similar flame in him. He had reservations about the course of his life. Yes, he excelled at his studies. Yes, he very likely would pass the licensing exams with high scores. No, he couldn't remember a time when he thought he'd become anything other than a doctor. But he questioned whether medicine was the "right path" for him. Almost inevitably, our conversation turned to my interest in initiating a conversation with the right brain by writing with the nondominant hand due to the startling results I'd seen other people achieve using the technique.

Albert agreed to try it. First, he surprised himself by getting two different answers to the question about what animal he might be. Next, I had him ask and answer the question:

Will I be happy once I'm a doctor?

He responded with the decidedly neutral statement, "I don't know." We talked about that answer. "No one can know the future for sure," he said. So I focused the time frame for him by asking:

Will I be happy when I've graduated?

He responded "Not really." In explaining that response, he told me he'd have to pass a series of licensing exams before he could practice medicine in China. We tried a third time with the question:

Will anyone be happy when I graduate?

And the "aha moment" arrived with the two words "my parents."

As we explored that answer further, Albert told me that his parents held the dream of their son becoming a doctor. In some important ways, Albert pursued this career track with incredible diligence largely because he didn't want to disappoint them. Once he opened himself to the thought, he realized that maybe another career path would satisfy him better than medicine.

By the end of the flight, Albert had resolved to speak with his parents about his feelings.

When we believe the lie "My life is as good as it gets," we simultaneously and systematically ignore the directly antithetical truth that "My life just isn't really all that good after all." But who wants to admit that? Instead, we push the contradiction out of our minds. If we don't see the contradiction, how can we take any steps to improve things? In fact, we may not have a clue about what we could do to make our lives better, but we're sure not going to figure anything out if we pretend satisfaction with the current state of affairs.

For both Albert and me, many years passed before either of us began to recognize the dissatisfaction and to question the underlying assumptions that limited us. At twenty-nine, he was a little younger than I was when I began to attend to my trouble with intimacy. The fact, however, that he was a little shy of thirty, while I had just passed that age, might have some significance. Though the two of us faced different circumstances, I wonder whether a person must live a certain amount of time before she or he can honestly assess life's limitations.

Without a doubt, this lie can be an especially difficult lie to detect. On the surface, "My life is as good as it gets" sounds positive. What could go wrong for someone who boldly pronounces that things couldn't be better? Listen a little harder, though, and you'll hear the ironic tone with which people usually say these words. They don't expect their lives to get any better. They've accepted the status quo and talked themselves into believing they'll get by if the current circumstances extend into the endless future. They live with the presumption that taking action to improve things will prove fruitless. Look deeply enough and you'll see resignation.

In circumstances where we believe we can do nothing to change the situation, we resign ourselves to the idea that it will never improve. (Or we may become susceptible to Lie Number 1, "Everything Will Work out Eventually," aka "Whatever Will Be Will Be.") But if the unchangeable situation is the course of our lives, becoming resigned means we must let go of our dreams. What's the big deal about that? Dreams are totally unrealistic anyway, reasons our logical left brain. Once stuck in a mundane routine, we expect nothing more. As with the story of waiting for "my ship to come in," this lie, too, positions the subject as a passive recipient of circumstances and forces outside his or her control.

TRUTH SERUM, DOSE 5:
"Could life be any better?"

Why do I so often have trouble believing I'm in the driver's seat of my life's vehicle? Haven't I learned the lesson that the more I expect from life, the better things will be? If I manage my expectations and pare them down to almost nothing, my life probably won't disappoint me much. But it may not make me very happy either.

Two things self-help books frequently suggest for coping with a downsized view of life: "Get a more positive attitude" and "Live today as if it were your last." If I could acquire a more positive attitude by simply flipping a switch, I'd turn it on every morning. What holds me back isn't my attitude; it's a lack of hope, the source of which I can't identify until I ask the right questions. As for how I "live today," if I feel more like a robot than a person, why would I care whether today were my last?

By asking the questions that focus my attention on the limiting belief, I can take the first step toward breaking free from it. When I ask, "Why doesn't my life make me feel good? or What can I do to make my life better?" I begin to loosen the trap that's making it impossible for me to step forward. When I look down at my feet or out at my life, as long as I only see the traps and impediments, my fear and anguish may make it impossible to see anything else. But what happens if I look again and see my life's obstacles as if they were my favorite pair of worn-out slippers? I love to wear them, even though they long ago lost their luster. Like the everyday routines of my life, it's hard to imagine anything more comfortable. Objectively, I know I should take the new pair I got last Christmas out of the box and throw the old ones away, but I just can't bring myself let go of the familiarity.

It is easy to feel at times like we are robotically

going through life. A friend, who was an Olympian rower, expressed it this way:

> "I remember rebelling against the Olympic rowing coach when he asked us to 'manufacture' identical strokes. The dehumanizing metaphor enraged me at the time. I guess I have always resisted being part of the machinery. Humans really can change in ways machines cannot. In spite of all this, I still do like team efforts. The T-shirt motto for the training experience was, 'No Pain, No Gain, No Spain, Barcelona 1992.' I guess I've always understood discomfort, pain, and struggle to be part of the path to greater things."

About a month after I'd returned from Hong Kong, I received an email from Albert.

> The last several weeks I have studied for the first of my medical licensing exams. I must memorize hundreds of facts about the brain. Thus, I am reminded over and over about the differences between the two hemispheres and that distracts me more than I would like, as I recall our conversation about right versus left hemisphere thinking.
>
> I've actually only used the intuitive writing technique once since we talked on the plane, but it helped me a lot. Before I spoke to my parents, I asked myself a series of questions that allowed me to clarify my life and career goals. When I told them I no longer want merely to practice medicine, my parents were disappointed, as I expected. But when I went on to say that I thought I would be

happier and could make a bigger impact on the general practice of medicine in China, if I used both my understanding of medicine and my scientific creativity in the medical devices industry, they understood.

So, that's my plan now. I'll finish my degree and the licensing requirements in order to become fully credentialed, but when I go back home I'm going to find a way to produce tools for practicing doctors. I return regularly to the revelations you helped me discover on the flight home. The discussion about my career plans evolved into more openness with my parents about the "independence issues" you and I spoke of. I guess I've had that subject on my mind subconsciously for quite a while. Thanks to you, I now think of my right brain as a personal psychiatrist that I can access any time I want . . . and its services do not come with a $150 per hour price tag!

As we've seen the implications of the lie that "my life is as good as it gets" contains the resignation that life won't get any better. That's a big difference from the notion that "I am truly blessed; my life is wonderful!" The latter statement overflows with gratitude. It expresses a bright perspective about the present and hopeful openness toward the future.

If you're subject to this lie, what steps can you take to ensure a brighter outlook? As I have indicated, subtle as it is, you'll need to work pretty hard to get underneath this lie. First you may need to overcome the hopelessness that asks, "Why bother?" If you've been living under the influence of this lie for most of your life, or if things have gotten downright worse recently, you'll need to climb out of that despair. The real issue underlying the existential questions about your quality of life requires you to discover the limiting factors— the traps, obstacles, and impediments. Are they more frightening than beaten-up but much-loved slippers? I've found it gets tougher to ignore the lie we're telling ourselves with the passage of time. Deep down we want our lives to be as fulfilling as possible.

Do you subscribe to this lie because you never went back to school, never quit the job you hated, never left the bad relationship, never made peace with a certain friend, coworker, or family member? Plain and simple, such unresolved stumbling stones require attention before any change can occur. You may talk yourself into settling for the version of life that gives you less than you'd like; it's easier than confronting what you must face in taking the necessary steps to improve the situation.

Your logical mind prefers to stick with the status quo because it's familiar and continues the line of your life. But the status quo cannot guarantee you'll never be bothered by another pesky question. Your left brain would rather that didn't happen, and when it does the left brain will do its best to review the situation and dismiss the question as quickly as possible.

Write the question:

What factors limit me and my life?

In your *Thought Revolution Journal,* shift your pen and follow the protocol to answer the question. Follow up with:

Is my life really as good as it can get?
Can I improve areas of my life? What are they?
What can I do to improve these factors?
How can I make changes?

Your answers may reveal a mixture of several limitations combined with factors you thought you had dealt with in the past. Unless you've managed to completely ignore your life's status, these answers may not come as a big surprise. On the other hand you could have an "aha moment" just as Albert did when he realized that the key obstruction to his potential happiness as a physician was not necessarily himself.

Like him, you may never have made the connection between the limiting factors and their full impact on your quality of life. Whether or not you make an illuminating discovery in the course of intuitive writing, simply to capture these issues "for the record" may ultimately prove beneficial. When you return to what you've written later, a clearer mind may reveal the profound accuracy of your assessments. If they lead you to life-changing decisions—as they did for Albert—so much the better.

THIRTEEN

LIE NUMBER 6
"EVERYTHING WILL BE OKAY."

LIKE THE PRECEDING LIE, THE NOTION "Everything will be okay" has a lot to do with settling for the status quo. Whereas "My life is as good as it gets" confines the lie to circumstances within a person's own life, the "Everything will be okay" broadens the situation to include factors and situations beyond the limits of "my life." For this reason it is the most insidious and least obvious.

We hear, "Everything will be okay" often in childhood. When problems arise, we gain some comfort by considering that things will magically work out without any added effort on our part. So when we hear, "Everything will be okay," we assume good outcomes. We need only to be patient. These thoughts often get us off the hook for taking any other action to remedy the situation because after all, the implication is, "Everything will be okay" anyway.

Many of the other lies we tell ourselves are related

to this one. Take procrastination for example. Why take action now if "Everything will *still* be okay," after you postpone it. Since this saying was ingrained in childhood, it is particularly embedded in our consciousness and will be consequently tougher to root out.

MEET BETH

Beth had just celebrated her fifty-ninth birthday when she lost her life partner in a car accident during a snowstorm. Like many gay and lesbian people her age, Beth had never openly acknowledged her sexuality at work. So although her coworkers knew Beth lived with a friend, none of them was aware that Ginny had virtually been Beth's spouse for more than eighteen years. Beth's company granted her a week of funeral leave, but that was the limit company protocol permitted.

When she returned to work, Beth graciously accepted the sympathy of her coworkers. She even took what, for her, felt like a risky step when she mentioned to several people that she would handle her friend's estate. Though at first her grief almost stunned her at times, Beth tried to work as though her life continued largely unchanged. After a couple of weeks, Beth's coworkers stopped asking how she felt. For the most part, Beth thought she had laid the loss of her companion to rest.

Two months after she returned to work, the economy forced her company to lay off four mid-level managers. Naturally, the company expected each remaining employee to pick up some of the extra workload. Like others, Beth felt grateful to have her job intact, so she wasn't too threatened when her boss asked her to take on some additional work.

Six months after Ginny's death, the work on Ginny's estate intensified because the potential tax burden would be reduced if the estate could be settled before the end of the year. Between her work as Ginny's executor and the extra burden at her job, Beth began to lose sleep at night. She no longer looked forward to her workday, and for the first time since they'd known her, Beth's friends listened to her complain about her job. In the course of a couple months, the complaints grew bitter.

Do you ever feel as if life has passed you by? Do you know that your situation feels very uncomfortable, but have no idea what other situation you might find more comfortable? Do you worry that spending too much time thinking about why you feel blue would only make you more depressed? Do you understand quite clearly how you arrived at the current state of affairs, but have no clue how to escape it? By indulging in the lie "There's always time to do it later," can you talk yourself into not taking any steps to resolve the situation today?

By accepting "This is as good as it gets," can you resign yourself to the hopelessness of the situation? Or, in a twist on the lie about not apologizing, do you wonder why you have to be the one to fix things? Do you even have any control over the situation? If you tried resolving it, would you achieve any material result?

I don't know about you, but Beth's answers to these questions would very likely cause depression. Perhaps you believe that your life is in God's hands or that you're on some predetermined karmic path. In either case, you conclude that you cannot—should not—attempt to control your fate. Surely these higher forces know more than you and, to the extent that they direct things, either "everything will be okay" or it won't, but no one can put the blame on you. Stay depressed long enough and you'll find it hard to imagine an approach to life that isn't fatalistic.

At the same time, when we strongly believe "everything will be okay," we gain some psychological benefit. Like most of the lies we've looked at, this belief quiets the mind. It allows us to suspend thinking about improvements to our lives. We get a pass from self-examination and self-analysis. We get the real-life equivalent of a "Get out of jail free" card. Our lives get a lot "easier," as long as we can hold on to this belief.

The idea that "everything will be okay" holds a lot of psychic resonance for most people. Think how many times someone has said these words to you. I'll bet your parents and grandparents said them to you while you were growing up. When you got a little older, you'd hear this refrain from teachers, friends, and neighbors. Pastors and counselors, doctors and nurses, lawyers and insurance adjustors—all use this turn of phrase. Typically, this reassurance follows shortly after some unpleasant occurrence, and almost always with the best of intentions.

But when I utter these words to my adult self in order to obtain the same comfort I got from others' use of them in my childhood, they become much less true. What truth these words contain, if any, resides in the promise of a future when things return to an "okay" or "normal" state. The sentiment behind them—offering comfort—rings true because we all need comfort in our afflictions. Yet, saying the words does not make it so.

Anyone who has ever grieved understands that the return of "normalcy" will come inevitably, but it does little to assuage the ache of loss that never goes away completely, no matter how much it diminishes and pales in the light of ordinary days. I wonder how many people older than seventy-five believe that "everything turned out okay with their lives." I'd like to ask how much they participated in making their lives happen or if "life simply happened to them."

Before you get too depressed by this thought, read on and learn what steps we can take with a dose of truth serum.

TRUTH SERUM, DOSE 6:
"Everything is NOT okay!"

Beth certainly couldn't convince herself that she was happy with how her life had turned out so far. And, whatever comfort she may have found in her co-workers' assurances that "everything will be okay" after Ginny's funeral, she couldn't find the truth in it even eight months later. After an especially angry series of complaints about her boss, coworkers, and job in general, one of Beth's friends introduced her to intuitive writing.

A couple of days later, Beth began working through the exercises in an attempt to articulate some of her complaints without troubling her friends. Beth asked herself:

Just what is my problem with work?

Her response was, "Work isn't the problem. I need to grieve." This admission took her breath away. Within the week, Beth joined a bereavement group. As much as she tried to believe that "everything will be okay," Beth's heart knew that everything was *not okay.*

When we catch ourselves saying, "Everything will be okay," we need to take a moment for reflection. I try to do that now, even when I hear myself say these words to someone else. Am I offering nothing more than false comfort? If so, I add some other remarks that I hope are more meaningful than the stock response. When I realize I've been telling myself the same lie, I know I need to take the opportunity to dive more deeply into the situation. I know the statement almost never covers the whole truth, so I want to investigate why I am willing to entertain it for the present circumstance.

Why are we ever willing to accept the status quo without also investigating our motives? Of course we need to believe that our experiences amount to something more than a whim of fate or a waste of time. Who could go on living if he didn't feel that his actions mattered somehow and that his life made some small contribution to others? This lie works because our rational mind uses it to convince the right "feeling" mind that it has permission to stand down. It insinuates that the situation needs no current action on our part because something beyond us will make it all right in the end.

If we developed both parts of our minds equally, we might not so easily convince ourselves (or one another) to accept whatever outcome eventually unfolds—expecting it to be "okay." How can we even the playing field a bit and allow insight from the creative mind to address the thinking mind?

If you find yourself believing the lie "Everything will be okay," take some time for a little dose of truth serum. Take out your *Thought Revolution Journal*, and ask:

*What is the "everything" that I imagine will
be okay in time?*

You may have a long list before you're done writing. Maybe you've taken on some problem at work or the relationship with one of your children, parents, or friends has soured. Maybe you've had some bad news from your doctor. Try to put down some reasons that complicate each of these issues. If you can identify obvious steps you plan to take to ensure that "everything truly turns out okay," get that information down alongside the particular issue it addresses. Write a thoughtful and honest assessment. The objective is to ensure that you are truly honest with yourself. Don't blindly assume things will work out okay. You can do this by questioning your assumptions. You will be able to get a second opinion, if you will, from your right brain. This process will give you a good reality check.

Now, let's turn the tables a bit. Maybe your intuitive mind can offer additional insights that haven't sprung to mind to this point. Begin with the question:

What in my world is not okay right now?
And then:

What must I do to make sure X turns out okay?
Of course, you should be answering these questions with your nondominant hand. Finally, write the question:

When is the right time to do X?
Did you gain insights that didn't show up before you started using your nondominant hand? Have you resisted thinking about some of these responses in the past? Before you conclude your work on this lie, you may want to expand your investigation to something more speculative. With your dominant hand, write:

Is there anything I can do something about right now to ensure a potentially better future?
If you commit to taking on these questions and following the protocol I've outlined, you may receive some unexpected insights, courtesy of your right brain.

FOURTEEN

LIE NUMBER 7
"I WON'T MAKE THE SAME MISTAKES AS MY PARENTS."

MANY OF US FEEL CERTAIN we know better than to follow our parents' examples. For a long time, we watched our parents carefully, so we reason that we know enough not to fall into the same traps they did. And yet, we often do just that. Three factors predetermine this likelihood: (1) We inherit our parents' DNA. (2) We are more familiar with their behaviors than most anyone else's. (3) If they did a good job raising us, we want to emulate the things they did right.

MEET BEN

Ben's father had been a very successful CEO in the aerospace industry. He put in long hours six days a week and, while growing up, Ben and I used to talk about not working as many hours as our fathers did. We camped, hiked, fished, skied, swam, and ran around together. What other fathers would typically do with their sons Ben and I did on our own. Both of us admired our fathers, their work ethic, their successes, and their sense of fairness and integrity, but we vowed not to miss out on sharing life's fun pursuits with our children.

After college, Ben went to medical school and specialized in internal medicine. Along the way, he didn't have time to excel in his career *and* focus on a relationship. Heck, I hardly ever saw him during his internship and residency! Then he went on to build his practice and establish his reputation. The habits he'd formed in med school followed him. He put in more and more time at work, eventually spending more hours between his office and rounds than his father did.

Guess what? I did the same thing—it just took me a little longer than Ben to get there. During my tenure at the bank, my hours grew longer until I, too, was working more each week than my dad had. Despite our best intentions, neither Ben nor I had lived up to our vow "to not make the same mistakes as our parents." The only "good" thing was that neither of us had children with whom we were spending little time.

Ben told me he felt sure he would remain alone all his life. From the time we were in high school, he'd no sooner start to date someone than he'd ask me how long I thought it would last. Once I asked him why he'd never found anyone. He responded that he just couldn't commit to someone who would eventually get bored with him and wind up going off with someone else.

It took me ten years of unhealthy work habits before my intuition nagged me to deal with issues in my personal life. Both Ben and I needed to improve our ability to function in relationships. Like Ben, I chose to ignore the message as long as I could. I had a handy solution: work more. I observed my father do it throughout my childhood and into the latter years of his life. In addition to engaging in the familiar pattern, I deemed my success acceptable. *Maybe I couldn't succeed at intimate personal relationships, but I had plenty to do at work,* I told myself. I threw myself even more intensively into my job because I knew from experience that success at work justified the necessary sacrifices.

Our parents have a huge impact on the way we lead our lives. For some of us, the tendency to believe that we are luckier than our parents probably derives directly from the effort they put into raising us. Because they did such a good job, we reap the benefits. Others believe that they know more than their parents because they recognize the inadequacy of the parenting they received. In either case, children do not escape their parents' role in their lives.

In my case, there came a day when I realized that I no longer accepted the compromise of career success at the expense of a personal relationship. In that regard, my parents functioned as great role models because their marriage has endured happily for more than fifty years.

TRUTH SERUM, DOSE 7:
"I can make my own mistakes."

Ben always managed to stay one step ahead of me. As kids, when we hiked or skied, Ben would lead. When we swam, he'd reach the dock first. When we fished, he almost always got the first strike. When Ben turned thirty-two, we went out for drinks. Ben was in a reflective mood and admitted how lonely he felt without a love relationship. When a partner joined his practice about three years earlier, Ben's career steadied and he started dating again. But none of the relationships worked. "I know I'm to blame," Ben admitted. "I'm thirty-two and have a one-hundred percent failure record in my love life. I think I find fault with every woman I ever dated because I'm afraid of intimacy. I've decided to find a counselor."

In one of his first few sessions, Ben told his therapist that he needed to learn whether he stood in his own way of finding someone with whom he could spend his life. The therapist suggested Ben buy Lucia Cappachione's book, *Recovery of Your Inner Child,* which teaches the technique of writing with your non-dominant hand. Not long after that, his intuitive brain reminded Ben of his vow "to not make his father's mistakes."

In his next session with the therapist, Ben revealed

how much it devastated his mother when his father left her shortly after Ben graduated from college. The next evening, as Ben worked through another exercise in Dr. Cappachione's book, his nondominant hand wrote, "You do not have to repeat your parents' relationship."

It took another couple of years for Ben to truly believe that he "could make his own mistakes," but he decided that learning to communicate, compromise, and commit to a relationship was a lot better than having no love life due to his determination "to not make his parents' mistakes." Today, Ben and Marie have six years of commitment behind them with one daughter and one child on the way.

Therapy worked for me as well, and in another of those synchronicities in my life and Ben's, my therapist introduced me to writing with my nondominant hand. What I learned was we must reflect on what limits us in life, particularly those obstacles we throw into our own paths or imagine our parents might have dumped there. We must learn to be responsible for our own actions by getting out from under either the positive or negative shadow of our parents to live our own lives.

Do you want to get beyond the lie, *I won't make the same mistakes my parents did*?

Get out your *Thought Revolution Journal* and write the statement there. Then, reflect for a while, listing whatever mistakes—your parents' or your own—spring to mind. Next write the question:

What mistakes did my parents make?

This time, answer the question writing with your non-dominant hand. Follow up with the question:

Have I made the same mistakes in my life so far? Why or why not? If so, how?

Then pose a third question:

What must I do to resolve this (or these) mistake(s)?

The process should give voice to intuitive, even creative ideas, which are typically suppressed by the thinking left mind. Don't become overwhelmed. Even if mistakes spill out of you that you would prefer to avoid, nothing will reveal itself that you won't be able to handle. Furthermore, it's unlikely these mistakes will catch you off guard. After all, these impressions originate with your longstanding observations of your parents and their impact on your life. Perhaps the amount you learn in just a few minutes may absolutely stun you, but I'd be surprised if the process turns up anything "new." At the same time, it could open the door to some incredible breakthroughs.

FIFTEEN

LIE NUMBER 8
"THERE'S NO SUCH THING AS TRUE LOVE."

AT LAST WE ARRIVE AT THE COMMON LIE that has afflicted me for most of my adult life. Since I was in my twenties, I've found it hard to believe that true love exists because I had never really experienced it. I managed to stay in relatively comfortable short relationships that bred familiarity, but after a while relationships would become routine and one of us would wind up taking the other for granted—leading to the inevitable split up.

Some of us believe that familiarity is a substitute for "love," but it sure doesn't feel very "true." Yes, we may like one another more than many couples do. We've listened to complaints from friends and family about the trials and tribulations in their relationships. We seem to have less trouble with one another than some of them. So maybe our relationship—with its mild disappointments—is "normal."

MEET BOB

Like my friend Ben from Chapter 14, Bob's love life had always proceeded quickly from one short-term relationship to another. He would tell himself he "just hasn't met the right person yet," but down deep he began to doubt the accuracy of that assessment.

Unlike Ben or me, Bob had dated many a woman with whom he initially believed he was in love. Yet, after a couple months, something always changed his mind about her. The problem could have been the size of her hands, the way she danced or laughed, or some other seemingly trivial issue. How could Bob go from "falling in love" with a woman one week to thinking she had too little—or too much—brains the next? The inconsistency and triviality of his complaints were undermining his desire to stay in a relationship.

Meanwhile, all around him, other people's relationships seemed to work—even if the two people weren't perfect for one another. In time, Bob began to wonder whether he had the problem, not the women he dated.

Many of us secretly search for the perfect partner while at the same time accepting the idea that we should stay in our current relationship because the "right" person could not possibly exist. As much as that thought is true in the absolute, when we half-heartedly maintain so-called "love" relationships out of necessity, resignation, or compromise, we can expect a lack of fulfillment, nagging doubts, and misery.

Social pressures, of course, motivate preserving

relationships over ending them—sometimes even when the relationship is rife with abuse. Ask any person who has made the decision to stay single whether he or she doesn't fend off various pressures to conform.

After Bob began therapy, he met Claire. When he told his therapist that he thought maybe she was "the one," the therapist asked Bob to make a contract with himself that he would remain with Claire for at least six months, which would be longer than any of Bob's previous relationships. Almost from the start, though, none of Bob's friends liked Claire (including me), and she didn't seem to like us either. Claire went out of her way to obstruct Bob's friendships. When we would all get together with our spouses and companions, Claire would invariably wife-bait.

Within earshot of whomever Claire had targeted at the moment, she'd tell the wife of one of Bob's friends the nastiest gossip she could dig up about another guy's wife. Claire seldom descended to outright lies, but when she did, she could do so with such poise that almost no one doubted her tales. More than one such gathering ended in tears and recriminations.

After an especially ugly episode, I invited Bob to lunch the next week ostensibly to discuss a loan for which he had applied at the bank. Actually, I wanted to ask him why he was still with Claire after all she'd done to hurt so many of his friends' feelings. That's when he told me the story about his therapist and the "contract." He really wanted things between him and Claire to work because he was at a stage of his life when he felt a lot of pressure to "settle down" and get married. As an aspiring politician, Bob thought he "needed" a wife. He felt pressure to conform to the public's expectations for political figures. He also learned from his father, who coached him in Little League and soccer, to "always give a hundred and ten percent; no one likes a quitter." Together, these stored messages wouldn't allow Bob to think about terminating this relationship, especially after so many previous failures.

Whether financial, familial, logistical, or otherwise, all of us make excuses for staying in relationships. Rationally, we prefer familiar routine to disruption and chaos. We typically want to avoid conflict. In Bob's case, however, he avoided conflict with Claire because of this "contract" he'd made with himself. All the while, Claire strewed conflict and disruption among his friends. Naturally, Bob didn't classify Claire's behavior as abusive; he simply thought she didn't like the other women. Yet, the greatest potential for conflict, as well as growth and change, comes from the person with whom we have a primary relationship. The deeper the connection and the longer the relationship, the higher the stakes. All too often, the unaddressed problems grow monumental and neither party can mend the relationship. Little wonder that so many relationships and marriages ultimately end.

Bob had told himself the lie "There's no such thing

as true love" for way too long. Lately, he'd worked with his therapist to disenchant himself of that half-truth, and they frequently discussed the hard reality about the necessity of "working at" any relationship. Bob really wanted it to work with Claire. In the past, he brought the problem into every love relationship in his life. This time, he couldn't imagine that maybe the other person was the one who had the problem.

Sometimes we settle for a comfortable relationship with a person we care about to avoid conflict and accept the status quo. To ease our right brain's sense of dissatisfaction, our left brain tells lies like "true love doesn't exist" in an attempt to sweeten the bitter pill we are about to swallow. Bob cared about Claire more than he'd ever cared about a previous girlfriend, and Claire certainly worked hard at keeping Bob comfortable, even if she upset all of his friends. Bob had grown accustomed to Claire, especially when the two of them were alone together—and that was happening more as time went by. The "exclusivity" of their relationship felt to Bob like it could be "love," since he'd never felt it with a woman before. "Maybe this is the way love is supposed to be," he told me during our lunch. I thought he was settling for something less than true love, but he had convinced himself that he might as well stay with Claire because he had slipped into another of the age-old lies (Lie Number 5). Bob now believed that the way Claire treated him was "as good as it gets."

Obviously, in Bob's case at least, such thinking made it easy for him to stay in the existing relationship. With these thoughts, he justified what I believe must have felt like less than a fulfilling relationship. I wondered, after so many previous break-ups pushed him into therapy, did Bob find it easier to stay the course with Claire than to admit that his first relationship since beginning therapy had turned out to be a mistake. Until this latest relationship, Bob's rational left mind discounted the existence of true love, while his feeling right mind urged him to find it.

Never before had Bob settled for an unsatisfying relationship, even if he had to make up the reason for feeling dissatisfied. With Claire, the tables turned. He'd lived with the belief that "there's no such thing as true love" for so long that his intuitive side adopted it and was willing to put up with Claire's abuse in order to maintain the semblance of a relationship with her.

TRUTH SERUM, DOSE 8:
"What does it take to fall in love?"

What could Bob do to open himself to the possibility of true love? I suspected that he couldn't improve his communications with Claire enough to make her see what she was doing to him and his friends. If he hoped to turn an honest eye on his relationship, Bob needed to communicate with himself better. During our lunch, I told him about my experiences with intuitive writing. After the introductory animal exercise, I suggested he write down with his nondominant hand everything positive about Claire.

To his surprise, he only came up with three things, all having to do with how she "took care" of him. Next I had him consider, "Have I found true love with Claire?" His left hand responded, "Just because you have never found it does not mean it doesn't exist."

I pointed out to him that he used the present tense verb "have." Did that mean he still hadn't found it with Claire? "Oh, my gosh! I guess it does!" he replied. Six weeks later, he and Claire split up.

Our lunch together, as well as Bob's consequent revelations to his therapist, helped him

Bob's nondominant hand response.

see that his girlfriend's problem was real and not made up in order to avoid commitment.

What can you do to open yourself to the possibility of finding true love? If you lie to yourself about the very existence of true love, how can you ever imagine finding it? Start by asking yourself the question Bob's intuition answered when his rational mind thought it was focused on his current relationship:

Does true love exist?

It's sometimes tempting to believe "I'll never fall in love." Let's ask:

What does it take to fall in love?

Refrain from applying the question to your current relationship, for you may not be as lucky as Bob and therefore divert yourself away from the underlying lie. Without switching hands, use your *Thought Revolution Journal* to record the question. Then try to capture as many of your rationalizations as possible. Allow your conscious mind to dump as much onto the page as it will.

To get the more intuitive perspective, transfer the pen to your nondominant hand and answer the question. Refrain from second-guessing or overanalyzing during this step. Later, you can compare and contrast the two sets of responses. In this way, you can differentiate between your experience-based, rational mind's thinking and your more intuitive, creative mind's impressions.

An interview subject wrote the following list with her nondominant hand in response to the question, "What does it take to fall in love?" "Open, trust, care, hope, light, luck, path, time, will, self-respect, respect, wonder, and laughter," she answered.

If you want to probe deeper, you can follow up with questions such as:

Is X the right person for me?
Am I truly in love with X?
Have I found true love with X?
Are X and I a good match?

These questions should give you some perspective about your current relationship, since your nondominant hand will reveal it in the light of a completely unfamiliar lens. If you aren't presently in a relationship—or even if you are—you may want to follow the initial Q&A with the query:

Why don't I believe true love exists?

If responses from the two parts of your mind confirm the existence of true love, you probably have a healthy view of love's potential, but haven't met the right person for you. I believe true love is not only possible, but is a natural part of the human experience. However, I also believe that, while we are all entitled to true love, many of us—including Bob—encounter issues and obstacles that preclude us from letting love happen. Short of therapy, how might you begin to deconstruct some of these barriers? Write in your *Thought Revolution Journal* about the clear and identifiable barriers you run up against. Don't neglect the question "Why?" Try asking yourself:

What things in my life prevent me from experiencing true love?

First, list your reasons with your dominant hand. Many of us so seldom tackle issues head on that sometimes sitting down to face a problem can provide a wealth of insight. Next, of course, you should answer the question using your nondominant hand. No matter how revealing your more rational perspective, you may be surprised by contrasts between it and your nondominant hand's responses. Finally, you may want to ask:

What steps can I take to attain true love?

Don't settle for the rationale that true love does not exist and therefore just accept the status quo. As self-defeating as this is, I have known many people who actually believe it to be the more sensible way. I've also known others—like Ben and Bob at the opposite end of the spectrum—who look for reasons to leave relationships, most times before they have given them a chance to succeed or fail in their own time.

We all have heard the stories of romance, of the couples married seventy-five years who died in each other's arms. Stories of love at first sight and friends turned to lovers are depicted in movies and books, and we admire the authors of these stories for giving us a glimpse of what others seem fortunate to have experienced. And sometimes, we are envious of the accounts of true love; other times they infect us and make us believe, or at the very least *want* to believe, that "true love exists."

As a recovered victim of impervious Lie Number 8, I am living proof that you can turn around this mind-set. Through intense work with my therapist and intuitive writing, I have opened myself up to the necessary risks in the name of believing in and finding true love. And as I suspected, my creative and feeling right brain knew all along where to lead me in order to work on the damage this lie had done to my heart and mind for most of my adult life.

Providing an outlet for my unconscious voice proved one of the most beneficial things I have done for all aspects of my life. I hope you will continue the journey I have mapped out for you, and I wish you all the love, joy, and success life—and your *whole* brain—has to offer.

ACKNOWLEDGMENTS

My own thought revolution may never have turned into printed form without the encouragement and support of many who inspired me along my path.

In writing this book I received valuable insights from the psychotherapy community, which included my sessions with Jeanne Harper, MSW, LCSW, and the book she gave me, written by Lucia Capacchione, PhD. Dr. Capacchione's book opened up the world of nondominant hand writing as the pathway to the right brain. Dr. Lauri Liskin of New York City provided a great deal of support and encouragement and the pivotal introduction to the publishing team in New York. Diane Gershman Levine MA, LPC, LCSW, provided helpful insights as well.

I'm grateful to Francesca Minerva and Ellen Ratner at Changing Lives Press for believing in me and the concept in this book.

A cadre of literary professionals helped me deliver the best product possible, including Bob Duffy, Steve Smith, an extremely talented editor, and Cheryl Laut.

Michele Matrisciani at Bookchic LLC, for her excellent judgment in the developmental editing process. Roberta Greene, for her public relations expertise.

It was essential to me that this book accurately reflects current neuro-scientific developments. Good counsel came from the faculty of Washington University in St. Louis through Dr. Charles F. Zorumski, Dr. Yvette Sheline, Dr. Andy Ziskind, former president of Barnes-Jewish Hospital, and Katie Compton and Nancy McKee at the Lifelong Learning Institute.

Further north, supportive friends David Dresner and Stacy Harris (who also gave me great notes) introduced me to the Neurobiology Team at the University of Chicago, under the direction of S. Murray Sherman, PhD. I learned from them. One team member, David Freedman, PhD, was especially helpful in ensuring I did not make any scientific leaps of faith.

Daniel Pink and Arianna Huffington both offered me early encouragement and motivation as a first-time writer.

Eleven St. Louisans stand out for the extra time and counsel they afforded me as early corporate world guinea pigs: Rick Snyder, retired senior vice president, Enterprise Rent-a-Car; Beth Davis of Clear Channel; Tom Boudreau of Express Scripts (retired); Norm Eaker of Edward Jones; Sister Lucie Nordmann, Head of School at Villa Duchesne; and Elizabeth Holekamp, Head of School at Thomas Jefferson School. My thanks to Eric and Mary Thoelke of TOKY Branding+Design; and to Kelly Hamilton, Elizabeth Tucker, and Damon Johnson of *ALIVE* magazine for entrusting me with their strategic thinking process.

Chris Ford and Nicholas N. Garza joined my creative team to help me figure out the next steps forward. Nick designed the book's mind-blowing cover.

My fellow board members and colleagues at Pulaski Bank provided me with the opportunity of a lifetime: to lead and develop a great company over a twenty-year period.

My family and close friends were early test subjects and like fresh oxygen over the years of this process. They include Mel Pashea, Mike Livingston, Joel Raznick, Karen Bolch, Michael Jernegan, Christy George, Kathryn Henneman, Steve Branstetter, Linda Wolff, Raj Tailor, Patty Wente, Jeff Kapfer, Rosemarie Fiorillo, Tim Bahr, Lance Davlin, MD, Amy and Amrit Gill, Julia Ruvelson, Robyn Berkely, PhD, Patty Fusco, Shahrdad Khodamoradi, MD, Jason Hall, Joan Malloy, Ken Haller, MD, David Hults, Scott Emmanuel, Ed Reggi, Betty Van Uum, Stan Mims, and my brother, Michael Donius. I'm grateful to the hundreds who agreed to be test subjects.

Art Baer and Charlie Colarusso were great mentors and friends, my grandparents, Sophie and Michael Burdzy, were always one hundred percent behind me and were no doubt rooting from above with my brother Tom.

My partner, Jay Perez, was a believer from the beginning and offered constant and steady support as I experienced my own revolution. He was my constant over the past three years. My parents, Connie and Walter Donius, are responsible for everything I've ever done right in the world.

INDEX

ABOUT THE AUTHOR

William A. Donius attended Tulane University's A.B. Freeman School of Business and Northwestern University's Kellogg School. His next thirty years were spent working in California and Missouri in the areas of management consulting, public relations, health care, television production, and banking.

Nearly twenty of Donius's thirty years in the corporate world were spent at Pulaski Bank in St. Louis, MO, where he led the bank through an initial public offering in 1998 and remained for an additional twelve years as chairman and CEO. During his tenure, the bank grew eight-fold to $1.4 billion in assets. Pulaski Bank was ranked one of the top performing small banks in the country by *SNL Financial*, voted Best Place to Work in St. Louis by the *St. Louis Business Journal* in 2007, and received a 2008 Torch Award from the Better Business Bureau for excellence in ethics and customer service.

During his tenure as CEO of the bank, Donius was involved in chairing numerous community events and fundraisers and served on the Regional Business Council, the board of the Missouri Bankers Association, and as chairman of America's Community Bankers (profit subsidiary). He was a frequent speaker at national banking industry conferences and a contributor to an industry publication, *America's Community Banker.* He also served as an adjunct faculty member at the National Banking School in Fairfield, CT.

In 2007, the *St. Louis Business Journal* cited Donius as one of the Most Influential St. Louisans. He also received the prestigious Volunteer of the Year Award in 2007 from the National Association of Philanthropy. In 2008 he was appointed to serve a two-year term on the U.S. Federal Reserve Board-TIAC Council in Washington, D.C. In addition he was the winner of the 2009 Equality Award for Human Rights Campaign in St. Louis and received the 2009 award from the National Conference for Community and Justice.

Donius has also served on a number of community boards, including the St. Louis Art Museum, Barnes Jewish Hospital Foundation, Maryville University, Forest Park Forever, and Area Resources for Community Human Services.

At age fifty, Donius chose to depart from the corporate world in order to devote full-time energies to his passions for writing, serving on community boards, and advocating for human rights issues.

Donius lives in St. Louis, Missouri, and invites you to email him at bill@WilliamDonius.com.